LANDMARKS OF WORLD LITERATURE

Homer

The Iliad

LANDMARKS OF WORLD LITERATURE – SECOND EDITIONS

Murasaki Shikibu: *The Tale of Genji* – Richard Bowring
Aeschylus: *The Oresteia* – Simon Goldhill
Virgil: *The Aeneid* – K. W. Gransden, new edition edited by
  S. J. Harrison
Homer: *The Odyssey* – Jasper Griffin
Dante: *The Divine Comedy* – Robin Kirkpatrick
Milton: *Paradise Lost* – David Loewenstein
Camus: *The Stranger* – Patrick McCarthy
Joyce: *Ulysses* – Vincent Sherry
Homer: *The Iliad* – Michael Silk
Chaucer: *The Canterbury Tales* – Winthrop Wetherbee

HOMER

The Iliad

M. S. SILK

Professor of Greek Language and Literature
at King's College in the University of London

CAMBRIDGE UNIVERSITY PRESS
Cambridge, New York, Melbourne, Madrid, Cape Town, Singapore,
São Paulo, Delhi, Dubai, Tokyo, Mexico City

Cambridge University Press
The Edinburgh Building, Cambridge CB2 8RU, UK

Published in the United States of America by
Cambridge University Press, New York

www.cambridge.org
Information on this title: www.cambridge.org/9780521539968

First published 1987, second edition 2004

A catalogue record for this publication is available from the British Library

ISBN 978-0-521-83233-5 Hardback
ISBN 978-0-521-53996-8 Paperback

Contents

vi   Contents

Preface

In assessing the *Iliad* as a literary work for a mixed, but largely
non-specialist, public, I have had occasion to discuss various issues
rather differently from the way that writers on Homer usually discuss them. In the process, I have said some new things about the
Iliad, which I hope will give the book an interest for the professional
Homerist, along with others. At the same time, I have drawn freely
on the ideas and researches of many earlier writers: among recent
studies, I would single out the books by Mueller, Mason, Vivante and
Griffin listed on pp. 100ff. I have also profited from comments on
the work in progress by Oliver Taplin, Malcolm Willcock, William
Wyatt, Jasper Griffin, Peter Stern and Terence Moore: it is a pleasure
to acknowledge these debts.

Note

Simple page references (as pp. 24ff.) refer to pages of this book.
Where modern discussions of Homer or the epic are referred to in the
text by an author's name (with or without a date), full bibliographi-
cal details will be found in the guide to further reading. Roman
numerals followed by arabic refer to the *Iliad*, by book and line: so
XV 20 means *Iliad*, book XV, line 20. References to other ancient
works are in general self-explanatory, but *fr.* stands for 'fragment'
and 'West' after a fragment number refers to the edition of the Greek
iambic and elegiac poets by M. L. West (*Iambi et Elegi Graeci*, Oxford,
1971–2). All translations of Homer (and other authors) are mine,
unless otherwise indicated. For this second edition, I have made
some small improvements to the text and have revised the *Guide
to further reading*. The overall shape and argument of the book are
unchanged.

Chapter 1

Homer's world and the making
of the *Iliad*

1 The *Iliad* and Mycenaean civilisation

Homer's *Iliad* tells of a punitive Greek expedition against Troy, led
by Agamemnon, king of Mycenae in southern Greece. The story is
set in a remote heroic age, distinct from and superior to the present,
in which war and warrior leaders are the norm. In historical terms
this heroic age is to be identified with the Mycenaean civilisation of
the second millennium B.C. (*c.* 1600–1100) and Homer's Greeks
(called 'Argives', 'Danaans' or 'Achaeans') with the Mycenaeans,
known from archaeological excavations at Mycenae and elsewhere.

The Mycenaeans were the first Greek speakers to establish a civilisation on Greek soil. Their ancestors had come from the north,
c. 2000, completing one of many prehistoric migrations under-
taken over several millennia by Indo-European-speaking peoples
from (probably) somewhere to the north-west of the Black Sea. On
their arrival they encountered a non-Indo-European 'Minoan' culture, which they eventually absorbed and displaced. The Greece
they then created seems to have been a coherent miniature empire
based on several palace centres, including one at Mycenae itself. It
was bureaucratic and centralised, although its orderly surface no
doubt concealed many divergencies, including new dialect group-
ings. Among its sophisticated features was writing in the syllabic
script now known as Linear B. Among its foreign contacts was the
ancient city of Troy, now Hissarlik in Turkey, situated a few miles
from the Hellespont and the Aegean sea.

In a period of widespread disruption throughout the eastern
Mediterranean towards the end of the second millennium, the Mycenaean palace culture, its bureaucracy and its writing, was destroyed,
c. 1100. In the same period Troy was destroyed too – more than

1

once – as the different layers revealed by modern excavation show. The layer known to archaeologists as Troy VIIa met a violent end *c.* 1220, which corresponds roughly with the traditional date for the sack of Troy (1184) accepted by the Greeks of the classical period. Whether the destruction of Troy VIIa actually was the event that lies behind the Homeric saga and whether, if so, it was the work of a Mycenaean force, cannot be proved or disproved. Both assumptions, however, are commonly made, along with the large qualification that the Homeric version of events is poetry, not history, and may well have little in common with the original enterprise, whose scale (apart from anything else) has surely been greatly enhanced in the retelling.

2 The Dark Age and eighth-century pan-Hellenism

The overthrow of Mycenaean civilisation was also the work of unidentified agents, but the most plausible theory refers us to the so-called Dorian invasion: that is, to an influx of as yet uncivilised Greek-speakers (Dorians) from the north. The aftermath of the Mycenaean age, certainly, was fragmentation and the establishment, over much of mainland Greece, of a distinct dialect group, whose various versions of Doric Greek (or strictly 'West Greek') persisted into the classical period and beyond. Faced with the new invaders, the older established groups sought refuge in remote parts of the Greek world, like the Arcadian highlands of central southern Greece, or regrouped to the east, or else migrated still further eastwards to the islands and coastline of Asia Minor. There, in historic times, the predominant dialects were Ionic and Aeolic, both descendants of the versions of Greek once spoken over much of the Greek mainland, and the latter now spoken where Homer's Troy had formerly stood.

These movements and migrations are known by inference. They took place in what we call the Dark Age – dark, because it has left us few traces, and because (partly on that evidence) it exhibits a cultural inferiority to the periods before and after, even though it is in fact the age in which iron was introduced to Greece. When, in the eighth century, the recovery of Greek civilisation becomes apparent, we observe a cluster of events which tell against the fragmentation of the Dark Age and imply a new sense of Greek identity, overriding tribal and dialectal differences. The organisation of the Greek world, it is true, is now based on the unitary city-state, the *polis*, whose independence is and remains its most cherished possession. The city-states, however, are now seen to share a consciousness of 'Hellenic' status (as it will soon be called) through their willingness to participate in common Greek actions and institutions. The climactic achievement of pan-Hellenism is no doubt the victorious struggle against the Persians in the fifth century, but its first expressions are already to be found in the eighth. In this century we note the inauguration of the first pan-Hellenic festival, the Olympic games (776); the rise of the Delphic oracle; and the invention and dissemination of a Greek alphabet from Semitic, probably Phoenician, sources. And in this same century Greece produced the *Iliad*: a work that celebrated the first known collective act by Greeks against an external power, and a work that offered all Greek speakers a common cultural point of reference, a view and version of the Greek gods that transcended local varieties, a standard pan-Hellenic poetic language, and a standard for – indeed, the very concept of – a national literature that was not simply the property of one parochial group. With the *Iliad* the pan-Hellenic ideal achieves a definitive form.

3 The date of the *Iliad*

The *Iliad* is to be dated to *c*. 730. This makes it the earliest extant work of Greek literature, and earlier than the *Odyssey*, also ascribed to Homer, and the wisdom literature of Hesiod. This dating, though widely accepted, rests on no early testimony. Thanks to the remoteness of the period to which the poem belongs and the comparative illiteracy of its culture, there is no contemporary information about its date either in absolute terms or in relation to other datable events.

Our dating is established by a combination of factors: the absence from the poem of any element that on either linguistic or historical grounds is definitely later than 700 or (if arguably later) any element that cannot be explained away as superficial distortion or trivial interpolation into an eighth-century original; the occasional occurrence in the poem of objects or customs (such as hoplite fighting tactics) which seem, on archaeological evidence, to imply a date no earlier than 750; late eighth-century vase paintings which *may* be representations of scenes from the *Iliad* (the most plausible is one on an Attic jug, *c.* 730, now in the Louvre, which has been identified with the events of *Iliad* VII, especially the duel between Hector and Ajax); a verse inscription on a jug from Ischia in southern Italy, *c.* 700, which refers to the cup of Nestor, described at XI 632ff. (but the cup might have been well known independently); linguistic evidence that, by a generation or so, the *Iliad* precedes the *Odyssey* and the *Odyssey* the poems of Hesiod, in combination with the ancient tradition that Homer and Hesiod pre-dated seventh-century writers like Archilochus and Callinus; and the consideration that, whereas seventh-century poets and even Hesiod, were known to posterity as individuals, 'Homer' to later Greeks was (like some relic from a remoter period) little more than the name.

4 'Homer'

Though indeed little more than a name to later Greeks, Homer was still regarded by them as a real person, not as some kind of legendary figure, like the singer Orpheus, for instance; and *Hómēros* is, at the very least, a real Greek name (attested, as a matter of fact, in Aeolic-speaking districts). Various localities laid claim to him. The most plausible tradition associated him with the Ionian island of Chios. A poem probably by Simonides (*c.* 500 B.C.: *fr.* 8 West) quotes a famous line from the *Iliad* (VI 146) and ascribes it to 'the man from Chios'; and it seems that a guild of 'rhapsodes' (reciters) called 'Homeridae' (descendants of Homer, literal or spiritual) existed in Chios at least as early as the late sixth century.

At all events, 'Homer' was the name generally associated with the *Iliad* – and the *Odyssey*. Here too, though, there was uncertainty. There were voices in antiquity that suggested different authors for the two poems; on the other hand, various heroic epics now lost (some of them dealing with parts of the Trojan saga not covered by the *Iliad* or the *Odyssey*) were often ascribed to Homer as well. If a late citation is to be trusted (Pausanias, 9.9.5 = Callinus, *fr.* 6 West), this was already the case in the seventh century, to which many of these epics must have belonged. At any rate, doubts expressed by the historian Herodotus (*c.* 430) about the Homeric authorship of two of these other poems (*History* II 117, IV 32) suggest that such ascriptions to Homer were current in the mid-fifth century. So too does a saying ascribed to the tragedian Aeschylus, that his plays were 'slices from the great banquets of Homer' (Athenaeus, VIII 347e). Many of Aeschylus' plays, extant or lost, dealt with known epic subjects, but it is apparent that he avoided reworking material from the *Iliad* or *Odyssey*. If the anecdote is authentic, then, 'Homer' for Aeschylus included at least some other early epics.

By the fourth century, however, 'Homer', without further qualification, meant the *Iliad* and the *Odyssey*. This is clear, for instance, from Aristotle's description of epic in his *Poetics* (chapters iv, xxiii) (although even there, the *Margites*, a lost seventh(?)-century mock-heroic poem, is still ascribed to Homer). Moreover, there is evidence that as early as the sixth century the *Iliad* and *Odyssey* were especially associated with each other and with Homer in contradistinction to early epic in general. In the first place, we have relevant testimony concerning the recitations of Homer at the great Athenian festival, the *Panathenaea*, at this time. From a variety of later sources we learn that one or other of the sixth-century rulers of Athens (the tyrant Pisistratus, or his son Hipparchus, or, less plausibly, the poet–statesman Solon) initiated legislation establishing the recitations and regulating their performance: they were to involve the epics of Homer only, and the epics were to be recited in full and in their proper order by a series of rhapsodes, with one ending where his predecessor left off. It is implicit in these accounts, the earliest of which belong to the fourth century (Lycurgus, *Leocrates* 102 and pseudo-Plato, *Hipparchus* 228b), that 'Homer', which did mean the *Iliad* and the *Odyssey* by that time, meant the same in the sixth century itself.

The same implication may be drawn for the whole archaic period – the seventh, sixth and early fifth centuries – from a different kind of consideration. Aeschylus was not alone in avoiding Iliadic and Odyssean themes, while favouring other epic material: this seems to have been general practice for writers from the seventh century down to the fifth, despite the accepted stature of the two Homeric poems themselves. This remarkable phenomenon is difficult to explain, except on the assumption that the two epics *were* distinguished from the rest, and from an early date, as specially Homeric.

We may conclude, then, that in the archaic period the name 'Homer', though often applied to heroic epic in general, was especially associated with our two epic poems, which were rapidly accepted as the masterpieces of the genre.

5 Do we have Homer's *Iliad?*

To speak, however, of 'our' two epics is to beg a large question: what is the relation between the *Iliad* (and the *Odyssey*) as we read it today and the Homeric original? This, in essence, is the so-called 'Homeric question', which has been considered and reconsidered for the best part of two hundred years.

The first printed edition of the *Iliad* was published in Florence in 1488. This and subsequent editions depend on medieval manuscripts (we possess about two hundred in all), the earliest of which belong to the tenth century A.D. These manuscripts in turn derive from a standard text, or 'vulgate', established by the scholars of Alexandria (Zenodotus, Aristophanes, Aristarchus) in the third and second centuries B.C. The Alexandrians' task was to collect and collate manuscripts of the two Homeric epics, then to produce a critical edition by rejecting suspect lines and choosing between variant readings. Besides their vulgate, they produced explanatory commentary on it (the basis of the marginal notes, or 'scholia', which accompany some of our medieval manuscripts) and also divided the two epics into twenty-four books each – one book for each letter of the Greek alphabet. In the fifth and fourth centuries B.C., the poems had been divided into different sections based on episodes: so Herodotus (II 116) refers to the 'exploits of Diomedes' (*Diomḗdeos aristeíē*), Thucydides (I 10) to the 'catalogue of ships' (*neôn katálogos*), Plato (*Ion* 539b) to the 'battle for the wall' (*teikhomakhía*). In the archaic period the poems must have been divided up for purposes of recitation, but on what basis is uncertain.

The effectiveness of the Alexandrians' editing is shown by ancient papyrus fragments of Homer. Those later than the second century B.C. generally conform to the vulgate; the earliest, which belong to the third century B.C., show remarkable fluctuations from it and from each other. So too do Homeric quotations in fourth-century authors such as Plato. It is clear, then, that in the fourth and third centuries the text of Homer was not fixed; and it is likely that this instability goes back to the fifth century, when (with the spread of literacy) the book trade was beginning to grow and copies of the epics, accurate or inaccurate, would have multiplied and circulated freely. Direct evidence for the state of the text in the fifth century is scanty.

For the sixth century, however, we do have evidence, in the shape of the traditions concerning the Panathenaic recitations in the time of Pisistratus (see p. 5). If professional reciters in sixth-century Athens were required to recite Homer in full and strict sequence, there must have been an approved text for them to follow. Where it came from is not known (perhaps from the Homeridae of Chios), but we may assume that a new copy was made, which will have brought changes to the text, if only changes of dialect. The Homeric poems as a whole have an intermittent Attic colouring of a largely superficial kind, which cannot have been original and is most likely to have entered the tradition at this point. Our Alexandrian Homer, therefore, is the descendant of a Homer Atticised for Athenian audiences in the sixth century, which was later disseminated throughout the Greek world in accordance with the new cultural dominance of Athens.

Were any other changes involved at this time? One major change is suggested by the ancient scholia, which tell us that book X of the *Iliad*, the Dolon episode, was originally an independent 'Homeric' composition, but was 'put into the poem by Pisistratus'; and it is certainly true that various participants of the episode (Dolon himself, the Thracian king Rhesus, the king's wonderful white horses which the Achaeans capture) appear nowhere else in the poem, and that, for this and other reasons, X is much more detachable from the poem than any other episode of comparable length (see pp. 34, 39). As against this, however, there is a Corinthian cup of *c.* 600 B.C., now in Brussels, on which a variety of Iliadic scenes and figures are depicted, Dolon among them; the implication is that the 'Doloneia' was an accepted part of the *Iliad* before the time of Pisistratus, who was tyrant of Athens, on and off, from 561 to 527.

Other suggested changes in this period are still more speculative. A late tradition represented by a remark of Cicero (first century B.C.:

de Oratore, 3. 34. 137) assures us: 'Pisistratus is said to have been the first to arrange in their present order the books of Homer that were previously scattered.' This might mean that Pisistratus initiated the compilation of an *Iliad* and an *Odyssey* from numerous short compositions which had never, until that moment, formed parts of larger wholes. The notion was once fashionable, and is embodied in the once fashionable name for the Panathenaic phase of the transmission, the 'Pisistratean recension', but is incompatible with the sophisticated unity and homogeneity of the *Iliad* (the *Odyssey* is not our present concern). In any case, it is very unlikely that Pisistratus, or anyone else in sixth-century Athens, could have done something so drastic to something so well known without (for instance) the learned men of Alexandria being aware of it. What underlies the tradition is presumably what also underlies the institution of rules for Panathenaic recitation: the two epics had indeed existed as wholes, but rhapsodes tended to recite single episodes. Pisistratus (or whoever) insisted on authentic, integrated performance from the new, Atticised text.

Our discussion of dating offers no grounds for positing any distinctive changes to the *Iliad* after the eighth century, our discussion of transmission none for any significant changes after the mid-sixth. It remains entirely possible that in the intervening period there were modifications, small enough and early enough to be *un*distinctive and therefore now undetectable. The nature and extent of such changes depends largely on the nature of the transmission between the eighth and sixth centuries: was there an authoritative text or, indeed, a text of any kind in the possession of the Homeridae then? Above all, when was the *Iliad* first written down? Here, as nowhere else, we enter the realms of speculation and controversy. There was an ancient tradition that the Homeric epics had first been transmitted orally (and therefore, presumably, composed orally) and were only later written down (so Josephus, first century A.D., *Against Apion*, I 12). This hypothesis has been widely accepted since 1795, when the German scholar F. A. Wolf inaugurated the Homeric question in its modern form by claiming (*a*) that the epics were pre-literate, and (*b*) that 'Homer' was less an author in the modern sense than a long, anonymous process of composition. The second claim, however, is misconceived, and (if the *Iliad* is to be dated to *c.* 730) the first claim is not strictly true. Widespread literacy, indeed, did not exist before the end of the sixth century; but informal inscriptions survive from the last third of the eighth, and it is reasonably assumed that the alphabet was introduced to Greece some decades before that.

However, the *Iliad* was almost certainly *not* composed by writing as we would understand it. Quite apart from any practical problems involved, with so long a work and writing technology (in Greece, at least) in its infancy, the compositional techniques visible in the poem are essentially oral (see pp. 14ff.). The poem, therefore, is oral in a newly literate age: it is transitional. A sign of this is the transitional status of its composer. Homer has a name and the beginnings, but only the beginnings, of a biography: he is to be contrasted with literate poets of later centuries *and equally* with his own entirely anonymous, and presumably wholly illiterate, predecessors. There is a correlation, then, between literacy and historical identity, and between illiteracy and anonymity. Homer seems to fall between the categories in one respect; it is our working hypothesis that he does so in the other.

As an oral poem, the *Iliad* does not presuppose our conception of a stable text over whose fate the author expects or demands absolute dominion beyond his lifetime. That conception is first explicit in the later archaic age. 'No one will change my words . . . these are the words of Theognis', is how one poet comes to articulate it in the sixth century (Theognis, 21–2). The early epic poet ascribes his words to outside agencies, the Muses. Well he might. In later, written, literature invocations to the Muse become a learned convention. For the composer of pre-literate poetry they sum up the limits of his proprietorial authorship. 'His' words were never strictly 'his': he cannot therefore presume to control them for ever. The opening words of the *Iliad*, 'Goddess, sing [me] the wrath of Achilles', signify a pre-literate outlook.

On the other hand, the remarkable bulk of the poem is an equally clear sign of the new literacy. In a pre-literate society literature must be performed; it cannot be read. In the case of a poem like the *Iliad*, performance means public recitation. The *Iliad*, however, is a 'monumental' composition about 15,000 verses long. In its entirety it would have taken several days of discontinuous recitation, as happened at the sixth-century *Panathenaea*: it could not, in any ordinary sense, be performed as a continuous whole. In a society that presupposes performance, however, there is something extraordinary about the composition of such a work. The natural explanation is that the 'monumental' composer was exploring: that he glimpsed the latent possibilities of the new medium of writing; that he saw in it an opportunity to achieve something of special value and a means of perpetuating that achievement indefinitely.

However, it does not follow that the *Iliad* was *composed* with any assistance from writing, nor indeed that it was committed to writing immediately or even soon. We assume that the concept of a fixed text, which the monumental composer's intuition had foreseen, created the pressure for a transcription: we need not assume that the pressure was translated into immediate action. The poet, if literate, *might* have written out his own poem, even though its composition was, in effect, pre-literate. He might instead have dictated it to a scribe: 'oral dictated texts' – not, admittedly, of such great extent – are known from Hittite and Ugaritic records of the second millennium. Or, on either hypothesis, the transcription might have been done in stages over a long period. This notion of the 'progressive fixation' of the text has been used to account for the incidental anomalies and inconsistencies observed between different parts of the poem (see p. 21), although such features are observable in most long works of literature to some degree and would be likely enough in any long oral composition, however transcribed.

All of these possibilities are open to the objection that it would have been difficult to transcribe such a long work so early (p. 9). An alternative possibility is that the transmission of the poem was in the first instance oral and that the transcription came later – in the seventh century? – when writing techniques and technology were more advanced. The immediate purpose of the transcription would have been an *aide-mémoire* for reciters (the Homeridae or whoever), and its product the hypothetical text used as the basis for the Panathenaic transcription in the sixth century. It is implicit in this hypothesis that large feats of memorising were for some decades required, but then so they were, for shorter periods, on any of the hypotheses discussed above; and we must allow for the impressive feats of memory characteristic of many traditional societies.

We must also allow – on any of these hypotheses – for the inexact-ness of the memorising involved. It is probably inevitable that *any* period of oral transmission would have involved incidental modi-fications. Minor anomalies might be created or indeed ironed out, wittingly (as the conductor 'corrects' the plain indications of the score) or unwittingly. Minor felicities, or infelicities, in the spirit of the original might be added. However, the difficulties experienced in proving that 'suspect' details (including details so designated by the Alexandrians) are 'late' or 'untraditional', as often alleged, sug-gest that modifications are likely to have been most common in the decades immediately following the original composition, when the currency out of which the poem's attitudes and expressions were developed will have been still generally available: they will have been Homeric in spirit, though not in authorial fact. The element of Attic colouring is no earlier than the sixth century. A few other incidentals may have accrued, or been lost, *en route*.

No doubt, then, in the strict sense we do not possess Homer's *Iliad*. But is there really any reason why we need worry the question any further? There is no prospect of our ever restoring the eighth-century original and *knowing* that we have done so; whereas it is quite possible that, even if we could restore it, we should prefer the *Iliad* as we have it. We continue, however, to invoke 'Homer', and not simply as a convenience: nothing that has been said makes the *Iliad* a communal creation, like a coral reef. But Homer's contributions and any from (let us call them) his revisors stand together. The qualities of the poem are to be assessed in their own right, irrespective of conclusions about authorship, mine or any others.

6 Oral poetry: performance and public

The famous poet [*aoidós*] was performing [*áeide*] for them, and they sat listening in silence. He told of the Achaeans' disastrous homecoming from Troy ... From her chamber upstairs ... Penelope heard the inspired piece [*théspin aoidén*] ... and in tears spoke to the divine poet: 'Phemius, there are many other histories of men and gods that poets celebrate to enchant mankind. You know them. Sit there and tell your listeners one of those; and they can go on drinking their wine in silence ...' But wise Telemachus answered her: 'Mother, why do you grudge the worthy poet

giving us pleasure as his mind is moved to? . . . It is no sin for him to tell of
the Achaeans' evil fate: people prefer the most topical piece they hear.'
(*Odyssey*, I 325ff.)

Never have I sailed over the broad sea, but only to Euboea from Aulis . . .
I crossed over to Chalcis for the [funeral] games of Amphidamas. . . . I
declare that there I was successful with a poem [*húmnōi*] and took the
prize, a cauldron . . . which I dedicated to the Muses of Helicon . . .
(Hesiod, *Works and Days* 650ff.)

The *Iliad* may be unperformable as an unbroken whole, but it
still presupposes performance. The original circumstances of performance can be reconstructed from descriptions in Homer (mostly
in the *Odyssey*) and the slightly later *Works and Days* in conjunction
with inferences from the epics themselves. Corroboration is available from other oral epic traditions, of which the best known is from
what was, until recently, known as Yugoslavia. However, there is far
too great a diversity of 'oral' types to give any one analogue, South
Slavic or other, a definitive value (see Finnegan, *Oral Poetry*).

The oral performer in the Homeric tradition chanted his words,
to the accompaniment of a stringed instrument, the *kithára* or
phórminx, conventionally translated 'lyre'. What he chanted was
a series of single verses ('lines' is obviously a very misleading term),
all formally equivalent to each other. The music (now entirely lost)
was essentially rhythmical support, but presumably also gave some
minimal melodic colouring to the verse. The performance no doubt
also included a measure of acting, but the word was the dominant in-
gredient. 'Song' is a common but misleading translation of Phemius'
aoidé.

The metre of Homeric epic, like all ancient Greek metres, was
quantitative: that is, based not on stress, but on patterns of heavy
and light syllables (commonly, but less felicitously, called 'long' and
'short'). The metrical unit, the verse, was based on the dactyl, $-\cup\cup$,
where '$-$' designates a heavy syllable and '$\cup$' a light one, and (as
often in Greek verse) '$-$' was equivalent to, and could replace, $\cup\cup$.
The single verse, though known as the dactylic hexameter ('six-
measure'), was not a stereotyped sequence of six dactyls ($-\cup\cup-$
$\cup\cup-\cup\cup-\cup\cup-\cup\cup-\cup\cup$), but a complex of alternatives, $-\bar{\cup}\bar{\cup}-\bar{\cup}\bar{\cup}-$
$\bar{\cup}\bar{\cup}-\bar{\cup}\bar{\cup}-\bar{\cup}\bar{\cup}--$, or, most commonly, $-\bar{\cup}\bar{\cup}-\bar{\cup}\bar{\cup}-\bar{\cup}\bar{\cup}-\bar{\cup}\bar{\cup}-\cup\cup--$,

i.e. a sequence with a recognisable cadence ($-\cup\cup--$) preceded by
a series of dactyls ($-\cup\cup$) or their equivalents ($--$). The verse was
thus a flexible but elaborately regulated entity, realised in various
rhythms, e.g.:

I 6   *ex hoû dè tà prõta diastétēn erísantẹ*
I 11   *hoúnẹka tòn Khrúsēn ētímasẹn arētêra*
I 130   *tòn d' apamẹibómẹnọs prọséphē krẹíōn Ạgamémnōn.*

Rhythmical variety arose also from a tendency to compose in groups
of verses, of which many would run on syntactically into the next
('enjambement'), and from the deployment of word-groups to produce breaks ('caesurae') at various points within the verse.

The performance was entertainment, hence suitable for a gather-
ing during or after a meal, but 'serious', artistic entertainment: even
the noisy banqueters in *Odyssey* I were expected to listen and concen-
trate in silence. Elevated festivals or games, such as Hesiod describes,
and less elevated public gatherings would have provided other possible occasions. Whatever the occasion, however, a work as long
as the *Iliad* could only be performed serially or in excerpts. Though
members of the aristocracy might perform for their own entertainment, as Achilles does (IX 186ff.), the performing poet was normally
a professional. He had a repertoire of different subjects, most of them
what Achilles 'sings' to himself, *kléa andrōn* (IX 189), the glories of
the legendary aristocracy. It is a possible, but not a necessary, inference that the contemporary aristocracy formed the basis of the
audience, as it plainly would for a court poet like Phemius. At all
events, Homer will have been but one of many performing poets,
each with his own repertoire and, perhaps, his favourite audience.

The oral performance was wholly oral: neither performer nor audience made reference to a text. Furthermore, every performance
was liable to differ from every other – in detail, arrangement, emphasis or length. It might, as a matter of fact, correspond closely to
an earlier performance, because the poet had memorised his material, or (less likely) some other poet's, and was able to reproduce
it from memory. It might, alternatively, be what the reproduced
version must once have been, *improvised* in whole or in part. In a
sense, any performance of a composition in any performing art is
always unique, and contains something that was not 'there' until

that performance. The improvised performance, however, is different in kind. It is not actually the performance of a composition. It *is* the composition, and by definition it is not a fixed entity. The size of the *Iliad*, which precludes ordinary oral performance, implies an extraordinary mode of oral composition. There is still no need to invoke writing, however, even if there is no way of ruling it out. What we should probably envisage is a long and developed poetic tradition, given to experiment, with much mutual awareness, competition, imitation and 'cross-fertilisation' between poets, and (on the part of one poet) prolonged experiment and practice, leading to the perfection, over many years, of a monumental work. In performance, that work becomes increasingly fixed and so, eventually, available for memorised transmission (more or less exact) to reciters. As Finnegan has shown, all of these processes (and even the possible intervention of writing) are documented in other oral literary traditions.

7 Oral composition: the formulaic system

One phase of modern Homeric scholarship begins with Milman Parry (1902–35). It was Parry's great achievement to demonstrate that Homer's poetic technique was fundamentally oral (that is, a technique suited to improvisatory performance); and to show that the oral-improvisatory technique involved a system so large and complex that it could not have been the work of one poet, but of a long tradition of poets. For the better understanding of such 'traditions', Parry then set out to investigate the still living oral poetry of Yugoslavia.

Parry called Homer's system 'formulaic'. Its function he saw in purely compositional terms: the system existed to make improvised composition possible within the strict metrical constraints of epic verse. A skilled orator or raconteur can improvise in ordinary spoken prose; to improvise in verse, especially in a strict metre, some system is required. Unfortunately, in emphasising the traditional character of the oral system, Parry misinterpreted oral poets as manipulative craftsmen rather than creators, even though it was oral poets who created the system itself. Moreover, by an arbitrary extrapolation from origins to consequences, he convinced himself and many others that the compositional difference between oral and written poetry somehow entailed that the aesthetic effects available to oral poetry must be different in kind – which for Parry meant that oral poetry was incapable of any form of stylistic richness, even a concealed cross-reference or a simple verbal surprise. For all that, his insistence that the system is an essential fact of Homeric poetry is soundly based. The Homeric formula deserves our attention.

Parry defined a formula as 'a group of words which is regularly employed under the same metrical conditions to express a given essential idea'. The simplest type of formula is a whole verse or block of verses which recurs elsewhere: thus the verse quoted above as I 130 –

> *tòn d' apameibómenos proséphē kreíōn Agamémnōn*
> in answer to him spoke lord Agamemnon –

recurs identically at I 285 and elsewhere. About one in eight of all the verses in the *Iliad* recur at least once elsewhere in the poem. They recur, when the context they suit recurs. Few of the contexts are conspicuous and few of the recurrences are conspicuous either, once we are attuned to the characteristic presence of repetition in the poem as a whole. In aesthetic terms, such repetitions are certainly limited in function, although not as inconsequential as Parry supposed: in conditions of oral performance, 'redundancy of information' facilitates on-the-spot comprehension; while under any conditions the cumulative effect of so many repeated elements is to convey a sense of overall regularity (see pp. 18ff., 88f.).

At the same time, we should note (as Parry again did not) that there are repetitions which *are* conspicuous, because the recurrent verses and their contexts are special. If we become less sensitive to ordinary repetitions, we become (if anything) more sensitive to extraordinary ones. For instance, the same three verses describe the momentous death of Patroclus at the hands of Hector (XVI 855ff.) and the parallel and connected killing of Hector by Achilles (XXII 361ff.): 'As he spoke, death's end came over him. His spirit slipped from his limbs and was gone to Hades, bemoaning its lot, leaving manhood and youth.' The passage itself and the two parallel contexts are striking, and the repetition unique. The same spotlight links the two moments: the result, inevitably, is a cross-reference.

The second type of formula is the formulaic phrase. Here belong
the 'stock epithets' familiar to all readers of Homer as concomitants
of common nouns, whether people or things. From a compositional
point of view, as Parry saw, such epithets must be seen together with
their nouns as distinctive metrical units which contrast with other
such units in a particular functional way. Take the hero Achilles.
In I 7 he appears in the nominative case as *dîos Akhilleús*, 'great
Achilles'; the phrase occurs at the end of the verse. He next appears
in the nominative at I 54, again at the end of the verse, but without any epithet. He then reappears at I 58 as *pódas ōkùs Akhilleús*,
'swift-footed Achilles', while at I 121 he is *podárkēs dîos Akhilleús*,
'fleet-footed great Achilles'; both phrases again close the verse. All
of these instances occur in the context of the plague on the Achaean
army and the quarrel between Achilles and Agamemnon that results from it. Within this sequence, Achilles is not appreciably less
great or less swift- (or fleet-) footed from one moment to another. The
epithets are each generic, in the sense that they point to Achilles'
permanent qualities, not to any temporary mood or activity; and the
noun-phrases they belong to form a system of equally permanent,
but metrically contrasting, 'equivalents'. Each of these 'formulae'
stands at the end of the verse, but each occupies a different metrical space, and therefore, in metrical terms, each completes a differently shaped beginning; and each recurs elsewhere in the poem
under similar circumstances. In schematic form, the relationship is
as follows:

Akhilleús	(I 54 +)	∪ − − |
dîos Akhilleús	(I 7 +)	− ∪ ∪ − − |
pódas ōkùs Akhilleús	(I 58 +)	∪ ∪ − ∪ ∪ − − |
podárkēs dîos Akhilleús	(I 121 +)	∪ − − − ∪ ∪ − − |

(where '+' denotes a unit that recurs elsewhere, and '|' the
verse-end).

Formulaic relationships similarly exist between units of identical
metrical shape but contrasting syntactic function, as in a pair like:

'black ship' (dative singular)	*nēì melaínēi* (I 300 +)	− ∪ ∪ − − |
'balanced ships' (accusative plural)	*nêas eísas* (I 306 +)	− ∪ ∪ − − |

Homeric ships are no blacker in the dative singular than at other times, and no more balanced in the accusative plural than at other times. For metrical reasons, neither epithet could be used in both contexts; accordingly, the two alternate, but on a systematic basis. These and many other sets of formulae are so constituted that there is formulaic coverage of several different metrical contexts, and yet rarely more than a single formula for any single metrical context.

Frequent as they are, the formulaic repetitions of verses and phrases represent only a fraction of Homeric verse usage. Parry and his followers, however, argued that though some Homeric verses might look more formulaic than others, Homeric verse as a whole must be overwhelmingly, if not wholly, formulaic in fact. The thesis involves the designation of a third type of formula, represented by innumerable word-groups which are in some way *analogous* to one another by conforming (still within identical metrical contexts) to abstract patterns of, for instance, grammatical structure. By this criterion, the following can be identified as realisations of one formula:

apéktane dîos Akhilleús	VI	414	'great Achilles killed'
ekékleto dîos Akhilleús	XVIII	343	'great Achilles commanded'
epeúxato dîos Akhilleús	XX	388 +	'great Achilles exulted'
*anéskheto dîos Akhilleús*₁	XXI	67 +	'great Achilles raised'

Each instance contains a familiar noun-epithet phrase as grammatical subject together with a verb. Two of the composite units recur elsewhere, but quite apart from that recurrence, the instances count as members of one formula-family, because the inconstant elements, the verbs, are grammatically as well as metrically equivalent: they are all third person singular, past (aorist) tense. The logical conclusion of this argument is reached when 'analogy' is said to cover the tendency of a single word to 'gravitate' to a fixed part of the verse and, again, the relation between phrases which are metrically identical and grammatically parallel, but have nothing else in common. Thus the pair

teûkhe kúnessin	I	4	'[it] made for dogs'
*dôken hetaírōi*₁	XVII	698	'[he] gave to [his] comrade'

would be accepted as formulaic blood-brothers, on the grounds that, besides their shared metrical disposition, they share a grammatical structure (third-person singular verb in past tense, dative noun).

Parry's theory is open to various objections. Many supposedly fixed and unitary formulae of the second type are actually mobile within the verse and subject to other modifications: the model name-epithet groups, therefore, are extreme rather than typical. Again, the more stable formulae of the first two types tend to occur at the beginnings or ends of speeches, scenes and single verses; in the case of single verses, the end is the normal place. Formulaic density, therefore, is concentrated, not evenly distributed. More fundamentally, 'formula' is suspiciously undefinable. Parry began by defining it as the fixed means of expressing 'a given essential idea'. 'Essential ideas' implies a crude opposition to what Parry called 'ornament', and that reductive opposition presupposes an untenable theory of language. Furthermore, the association of formula and 'essential idea' is incompatible with those instances of analogy (some discussed by Parry himself) where phrases appear to belong together by association of sound not sense, as with:

(en) píoni démōi	XVI	437 +	'(in) a rich land'
(boûn) . . . píona dēmōi	XXIII	750	'(ox) rich in fat'

On reflection, it is obvious that the whole class of formulae by analogy is barely relatable to 'essential ideas' at all.

If 'essential ideas' pose such problems, might the solution lie in giving more weight to 'analogy', as Parry himself increasingly did? After all, formulae must be invented once and first used once, and on its first use a formulaic phrase can only be (at most) a formula by analogy. Perhaps the formula by analogy, not the fixed formula, is the original type and, thereafter, the representative type. This may indeed be true – but it is no solution. If 'analogy' is to be representative, it must fit most, even all, of Homer's verse usage; but if it is to fit most, let alone all, of Homer's usage, 'analogy' must be conceived so broadly that it includes what all poets of all eras are wont to do: compose in metrical patterns. It would be impossible to imagine a more complete verbal inventiveness than Shakespeare's; yet even in the English blank verse line, which is vastly less constricting than Homer's hexameters, Shakespeare can be seen to be composing in metrical patterns. Take, for instance, a set of instances from *Antony and Cleopatra*, which involve a favoured three-syllable cadence to close the line, notionally stressed / x / (where '/' marks a stressed syllable and 'x' an unstressed). The cadence consists of three monosyllables: first a pronominal subject (or equivalent implied), then an auxiliary verb, then a finite verb. There follows the finite verb's object, or a dependent phrase, or some other equivalent, in enjambement at the beginning of the next line:

thou didst drink	The stale of horses
I shall break	The cause of our expedience
and will make	No wars without doors
and did want	Of what I was
she did lie	In her pavilion
thou must know	'Tis not my profit
you did know	How much you were my conqueror
I will seek	Some way to leave him
and have fought	Not as you served the cause
you shall find	A benefit in this change.

The point is not that here Shakespeare is composing in 'formulae', but that when Homeric verse does what Shakespearean verse does here, there is no reason to invoke 'formulae' at all. Homer, it may be, composes in such patterns more extensively. The point is not affected.

The clear implication of this argument is that we should identify formulae only in the contrastive systems and the fixed, stable, repeated phrases or verses such as do *not* occur in fully literate poetry like Shakespeare's. Accordingly, we must accept that Homeric verse is part formulaic and part not; or rather that it embodies a spectrum from fixed, repeated elements, through contrastive systems and clear-cut parallel structures, to 'free' composition – that is, as free as strict metrical constraints permit.

As a modern analogy to the coexistence of these different elements we might consider the limerick. In this admittedly trivial (but also sophisticated) form, we have a given five-line metrical structure, a given rhythm within each line, and a given rhyme scheme. Provided it complies with these restrictions, the verbal contents of the limerick are notionally free. In general, however, the opening words of the whole structure conform to one of a few set patterns, notably

> There was a(n) *a b* of *c*
> Who . . .

where *a* is a monosyllabic adjective (often 'young' or 'old'), *b* a noun like 'man', 'girl', 'person', and *c* a place. In the original versions of the limerick, its inventor, Edward Lear, tended to finish the sequence with a fifth line echoing the first and repeating its rhyme-word:

> That *x a b* of *c*.

Hence, e.g.:

> There was an old man of Hong Kong,
> Who never did anything wrong;
> He lay on his back
> With his head in a sack,
> That innocuous old man of Hong Kong.

The more fixed elements of the limerick serve as a base, a springboard or a homing-point for the more free. The same may be said of Homeric verse. A convenient example is the first verse of the *Iliad*, convenient partly because Parry himself chose I 1–25 as a representative sample for formulaic analysis:

> *mênin áeide theà Pēlēïádeō̜ Akhilêos*
> wrath 'sing', goddess, of Peleus' son Achilles
> 'goddess, sing the wrath of Achilles, son of Peleus'

The name-epithet phrase *Pēlēïádeō̜ Akhilêos* recurs elsewhere at the end of the verse (I 322 etc.): it is a set formula. The word *mênin* recurs *once* in all Homeric epic in the same position (the start of the verse) and in the same syntactical relationship with a genitival phrase at the end of the verse (XVI 711 *mênin . . . hekatēbólou Apóllōnos*, 'the wrath . . . of archer Apollo'). This is one of the types of parallel structuring that Parry identified as formulaic, and that we should not. The rest of the verse, even on the most generously conceived Parryan principle of 'analogy', is free. Some parts of the *Iliad* are more visibly formulaic than this verse, some are less. The texture of the whole epic embodies a perpetual oscillation between the fixed and the free, with important aesthetic consequences (see pp. 48ff., 56ff.).

8 Oral composition: conclusions

If the oral-improvisatory basis of Homeric epic helps to explain the *Iliad*'s repetitions, it also sheds light on two other features of the poem, its anomalies and its stereotyped scenes. In the first place, the *Iliad* (in Mueller's words) is 'magnificently designed and poorly edited'. Its overall organisation is impressive and sophisticated, its detail sometimes trivially disorganised. For instance: the poem begins with a ransom and an argument (I), a ceremonial aggregation of forces (II), and an important single combat (III), and ends, symmetrically, with a still more important single combat (XXII), another ceremonial aggregation (XXIII), and another ransom and a reconciliation (XXIV). On the other hand, this same poem includes a carefully described embassy to the embittered Achilles which seems at first to consist of three named members (IX 168–9), then of two (IX 182–200), and then again of the original three (IX 222ff.). We may overlook the fact that a minor hero, Pylaemenes, is killed at V 576ff., yet is still alive at XIII 658; we do tend to notice that the armour Hector strips off the dead Patroclus (XVII 125) had already been removed by Apollo before Patroclus' death (XVI 793–804). Such minor anomalies are the result of a mode of composition distinct from those associated with habitual writing and reading. An oral composer may develop a new idea, but too late to prepare for it. He may combine two different ideas, scenes, variations on a theme, without removing all the inconsistencies between them. In oral performance, neither author nor audience can go back; and the habits of expression developed in such an oral *milieu* are carried over into the *Iliad*, whatever its precise relation to literacy.

The *Iliad* portrays many moments of action. Of the moments portrayed, many, especially incidental moments, are more like other such moments elsewhere in the poem than our experience of later literature, and perhaps of life itself, would lead us to expect. Scenes of many kinds – from assemblies to dreams, from meals to combats – tend to show a lack of individuality which is reminiscent of the generic epithet systems on a larger scale and which, like them, invites reference to the oral-improvisatory conditions of epic composition. The composer has at his disposal a range of 'typical' thematic material, as well as sets of formulaic equipment, on which he may support his composition and with which he may guarantee its improvisatory fluency. As a consequence, we may, if we choose, analyse much (though not all) of the *Iliad* into 'a limited number of standardised modular components'. But such analysis, in itself, is not a description of the epic: 'What literary critic would confuse a poem with a dictionary of its words?' (Both points are Mueller's.) Some highly literate traditions of poetry involve comparable restrictions. The rigorous, self-imposed limitations of vocabulary and idiom in Racinian tragedy of the seventeenth century offer one parallel. And in the *Iliad* (as in Racine) 'standardisation of components' is not some isolated feature of the poetry: it is closely related to other aspects of Homer's composition and, along with those, it has a positive significance of its own (see pp. 58–60, 88).

Homeric poetry is open to many analogies, all more or less partial, and inevitably it looks different according to the analogy chosen. Analogy with South Slav epic makes Homer seem alien and crude. My limerick comparison tends to trivialise Homer instead, which is at least not the effect of comparison with Racine. One quite different kind of analogy is worth noting, perhaps a surprising one. If Homeric art is oral-improvisatory, we may gain a valuable perspective on it from the only developed improvisatory art that is native to the modern Western world, namely jazz. Any performer or student of jazz could have told Milman Parry something about oral composition, its products and its practitioners: the creative individuals who learn their craft from a living tradition of fellow-artists in a *milieu* of mutual respect, personal ambition and restless experiment. Moreover, an understanding of jazz might have saved Parry from some of his gratuitous assumptions. Jazz was improvisatory when it began and, in all its many varieties, has remained essentially improvisatory – and yet musical literacy has been absorbed into it for over two full generations. The jazz soloist, in particular, may improvise his performance; he may have memorised it, in whole or part, from an earlier performance or from practice or even from a score, composed by himself or an arranger; he may read the solo from such a score: the same solo might result. In some idioms of jazz, the improvising soloist does little more than play variations on a pre-existing theme, and those variations rely largely on standardised melodic and rhythmic components. In other idioms, an improvisation, even on 'the same' theme, may strip the melody down to its underlying harmonic logic and from that base develop an entirely new melodic sequence. We have here a clear equivalent to a more and a less standardised – formulaic or thematic – mode of poetic composition.

The knowledge that Homeric epic is oral-improvisatory carries in itself no implication for its interpretation or assessment. As the jazz analogy suggests, from the origins of a performance (improvised? rehearsed? remembered? read? some combination?) we cannot predict the effect. In art, process and product cannot be mechanically correlated; and the quest, associated with Parry and his followers, for a distinctive 'oral poetics' is a wild goose chase. The oral aspect of the *Iliad* is a *datum* which we must take into account; but our own findings while reading and re-reading are our primary *data*, which no preconceived theory about oral poetry can contradict.

9 The language of the *Iliad*

Homeric Greek is a strange linguistic composite. Although mainly archaic Ionic, it contains words and forms of words from several different periods and dialects. We find, for instance, three different forms for the word 'feet' in the dative case: *posí(n)*, which is contemporary Ionic, *possí(n)*, which is archaic Ionic, and *pódessí(n)*, which is Aeolic. Or again: the contemporary form for masculine singular nouns of the second declension in the genitive case was *-ou*, the archaic form *-oio*: Homer uses both. It is as if, in English usage, the formal 'it is', the archaic ''tis' and the colloquial 'it's' could alternate without distinction within the same poetic vocabulary. From a compositional point of view, the great advantage of such equations is that they increase the range of metrically different alternatives: for instance, *posí(n)*, *possí(n)*, *pódessí(n)* contrast as $\cup\bar{\cup}, -\bar{\cup}, \cup-\bar{\cup}$.

The linguistic composite is used as an undifferentiated entity: we do not find archaisms or dialectal features exploited for their archaic or dialectal flavour in particular contexts. The dialect mixture doubtless reflects the prehistory of the epic tradition, though in what way is not entirely clear. The presence of archaisms is certainly attributable to the long poetic tradition behind Homer that the formulaic system requires us to assume (see pp. 14, 61). Not surprisingly, notable archaisms are often embedded in formulaic phrases themselves, whereas some elements in Homer's verse – for instance, the famous epic similes – seem relatively 'modern'. It has been inferred that the more 'modern' elements may embody more of Homer's personal inventiveness. As elements in the *Iliad*, however, they are no more and no less 'Homeric' than any others.

10 Society in the *Iliad*

Like Homeric language, Homeric society defies any attempt to relate it to a particular historical reality. Set in a remote heroic age, the world of the *Iliad* is a sophisticated fiction, with elements derived from different traditions and memories, different periods and localities, and other elements purely imaginary. The most obvious symptom of the poem's unhistoricity is the impossible scale of the achievements and activities that it depicts: the huge wealth of Troy and the huge Achaean expedition are no more historical than the huge physical strength of the heroes, which permits them to cast weights such as 'two men of today' could not even lift between them (XX 285ff.). Heroic hugeness is contrasted with the mundane here and now, and the contrast is primarily a symbolic one.

Some of the memories embodied in the *Iliad* do indeed go back to the Mycenaean age: even some particular objects, like Nestor's cup (XI 632ff.). Then there are negative recollections: the epic avoids anachronistic allusion to the post-Mycenaean migrations of Dorians from the north and Ionians to the east. But fictional re-interpretation is generally detectable. The chariot is remembered as the Mycenaean fighting machine; but instead of the weapon it was, it has become a transport vehicle. Bronze is remembered as the Mycenaean metal for weaponry; but iron, which belongs to a later age, serves in Homer as the metal for ordinary tools. The *Iliad* preserves the tradition of the Mycenaean palace centres and their actual locations, at Mycenae and elsewhere, but gives no hint of the sophisticated administrative system, the bureaucracy, and the writing, on which the palaces depended. Homer's warrior heroes may live, in some ways, like warlords of the second millennium; but when they die, they are not buried, as their Mycenaean counterparts would have been, but cremated like men of Homer's own era.

The values and the social institutions of the *Iliad* are certainly, on the whole, post-Mycenaean – and generally, perhaps, a poeticised version of the realities of the Dark Age immediately before the poet's own time. The basis is aristocratic. There is a stratification between the warrior aristocracy (at the head of which, *primus inter pares*, is one man, like Agamemnon) and the mass of free peasants and occupationally defined types, who may enjoy some kind of citizen status but 'count for nothing in war or council' (II 202). There is the institution of guest-friendship, whereby the aristocrats exchange hospitality and gifts: the beneficiary gains honour, the benefactor gains the other's future support. This institution is taken seriously: hence Glaucus and Diomedes, though only the descendants of guest-friends, refuse to fight (VI 215ff.); hence, too, the outbreak of the Trojan war itself, the result of a breach of the code when Paris, though a guest of Menelaus, stole his wife Helen (XIII 620 7). Above all, there is the individualist ethic to which the aristocratic heroes subscribe: their concern for personal honour (*timé*) and their competitive ambition 'always to be best' (VI 208). That 'best', however, implies mutual recognition. Theirs is not an outlook in which conscience and internal moral sanctions bulk large. The chief sanction that they recognise is the risk of losing face with their peers. Theirs is a 'shame culture', not a 'guilt culture'.

The lifestyle and the socio-political basis of this aristocratic existence are presented as reality in the *Iliad*. For us as readers it is sufficient to know that diverse materials have been fictionalised into a homogeneous composite within which the whole Greek world is presented as a social and material uniformity. The historicity of the component parts of this new whole is by the way.

11 The religious background

By comparison with the well-known world religions, the polytheism of early Greece was untidy and unsystematic, without sacred texts, an organised priestly caste, or specialist theologians to reduce it to order. Combining diverse elements from Mycenaean, Minoan and

Near Eastern sources – Indo-European and non-Indo-European – it existed in innumerable separate localised cults of its many different deities. The Iliadic version of this religion is once again a distinctive construct, not a reproduction of any particular phase or local tradition. Nevertheless, there is still a recognisable continuity between it and the religion of later Greece: it is no mere literary apparatus, but a 'real' religion, believed in by the Greeks who believed in it, although (as befits a culture of external morality) not to be defined in terms of belief. Herodotus (II 53) offered the opinion that 'Hesiod and Homer' had a formative role in creating Greek religion as the fifth century knew it, which is to say that the epic treatment of the gods and human responses to the gods had a lasting impact, not only on literature, but outside the literary sphere altogether. This is sufficient demonstration of the 'reality' of Homeric religion, as seen from a fifth-century standpoint.

The gods of the *Iliad* have an independent existence which is accepted without question by all the characters and assumed by the narrative. They are articulated as rational, comprehensible, anthropomorphic beings, separate from men and from one another, each with his or her individual temperament, sphere, and attributes, which are expressed in mythical terms more striking for their lucidity than for the mystery or irrationality associated with the myths of many other cultures. These gods are largely amoral, 'beyond good and evil' (as Nietzsche puts it in *The Birth of Tragedy*). They concern themselves with men in general, but take a special interest in the Greeks; and they are conceived of as pan-Hellenic deities, living together in a divine community on Mount Olympus. Whereas Greek cult gave each deity a multitude of local habitations, associated with local traditions, in different earthly sites, Homeric religion transcends local variations in myth and in cult.

The most important difference between Homeric religion and the non-literary religion of its age will have been the aristocratic character of Homer's gods. They support and inspire the aristocratic heroes, and they do this because they are like them. Their sociology and their psychology parallel those of the heroes. Like the heroes, they guard their individual honour jealously, they feud with each other, but they accept each other as peers, and also accept Zeus as their overlord, first among equals, as Agamemnon is accepted among the Achaeans. As such, however, they represent a special development of one side of Greek religion, one which is developed at the expense of a whole area of 'popular' religious experience. The Olympians live above us in the clear light. Alongside their worship, in the Greek communities, there existed darker and, in some ways, deeper cults of fertility, death, ancestor worship ('hero' cults in the strict sense) and ritual ecstasy. From the epic we would never dream of the power exercised over ordinary people in all periods of Greek history by mystery religion, by the 'chthonic' powers of the soil, or the realms beneath the soil, by everything that Nietzsche called the 'Dionysiac' in contradistiction to Homer's 'Apolline' pantheon; and indeed in the *Iliad* the ecstatic Dionysus himself is not even mentioned, except incidentally (VI 132ff., XIV 325). The popular cults offered mystical hope or comfort, they paid less heed to social distinctions, they might even subvert them. Religion is central to the *Iliad*, and the tacit suppression of these cults is central to the poem's religious orientation.

Chapter 2

The poem

12 Summary

The *Iliad* assumes a series of events preceding the action it describes, especially the abduction of Menelaus' wife, Helen, by Paris, son of Priam, the king of Troy, and then the subsequent organisation of an Achaean expedition against Troy, commanded by Menelaus' brother, Agamemnon. Along with Agamemnon and Menelaus, the Achaean chieftains include Ajax, son of Telamon, Diomedes, Odysseus, the old counsellor Nestor, and the greatest of all the Achaean warriors, Achilles, and his friend and ally, Patroclus. The most important figures on the Trojan side are Priam and the rest of the royal household: Hecabe, Priam's wife; the pair who caused the war, Helen and Paris; Hector, brother of Paris and leader of the Trojan forces; and Andromache, Hector's wife. Among the other notable Trojan heroes is Aeneas, son of the love-goddess Aphrodite, who is herself active on the Trojan side. Other deities likewise support one of the opposing armies. Like Aphrodite, Apollo, god of ritual purity, and Ares, the war-god, assist the Trojans, whereas Athene, the sea-god Poseidon and Zeus' consort, Hera, support the Achaeans. Zeus himself, king of the gods, intervenes on both sides at different times, without such partiality.

The main events presented in the poem are as follows:

I In the tenth year of the Trojan war, the Achaean expeditionary force, with its ships and men, is established on the shore near Troy. Agamemnon has offended Chryses, a priest of Apollo, by refusing to let the priest ransom his daughter Chryseis, Agamemnon's slave. As punishment, Apollo sends a plague on the Achaeans. At a special assembly, Agamemnon agrees to give the girl back, but, as compensation, takes Briseis, Achilles' concubine. Feeling himself dishonoured, an angry Achilles, with Patroclus and all their forces, withdraws from the war and appeals to his goddess-mother Thetis, who persuades Zeus to avenge him by supporting the Trojans. An argument at once breaks out between Zeus and the Achaeans' helper, Hera, but is settled by Hera's son, the craftsman-god Hephaestus.

II Agamemnon dreams that he will at last take Troy, and tests his army by proposing that they return to Greece. The proposal misfires, when the troops rush to get ready for home. Despite an intervention by the upstart Thersites, Odysseus restores order, and the army is mobilised. A catalogue of the Achaean and Trojan forces follows.

III The two armies advance onto the plain outside Troy, but agree to a truce: Paris and Menelaus are to fight a duel for Helen. On the walls of Troy, Helen points out the Achaean leaders to Priam. In the duel Paris is saved from defeat by Aphrodite, who takes him back to Helen inside the city.

IV Hera's hostility to Troy induces the gods to have the truce broken. Athene persuades Pandarus, one of the Trojans' Lycian allies, to shoot at Menelaus, who is lightly wounded. General fighting begins.

V With Athene's assistance Diomedes wreaks havoc among the Trojans and even assaults Aphrodite, when she tries to rescue Aeneas, and Ares, when he rallies the Trojan forces.

VI Diomedes' momentum is checked when he finds himself confronting a guest-friend, the Lycian Glaucus: the two decline to fight each other. Leaving the battlefield, Hector goes back to Troy to arrange with Hecabe an offering to Athene for her favour. While there, he speaks to Helen, then to Andromache (with their baby son Astyanax), and rebukes Paris who eventually re-emerges for the fight.

VII Hector and Paris return to the battlefield. Hector challenges one of the Achaeans to a duel. Ajax is chosen as his opponent, but the duel is indecisive. A truce for the burial of the dead is arranged, during which, on Nestor's advice, the Achaeans fortify their camp.

VIII Forbidding the other gods to interfere in the fighting, Zeus gives encouragement to the Trojans. After a day's fighting, the Achaeans withdraw behind their fortifications, while the Trojans camp on the plain.

IX Concerned at the Trojan advance, Agamemnon acts on a suggestion by Nestor that Ajax and Odysseus, together with Achilles' old tutor Phoenix, be sent to appease Achilles. Achilles is offered handsome requital (his girl back, one of Agamemnon's daughters in marriage, and generous gifts as well), but rejects it, and the embassy returns in failure.

X During the night, acting on another of Nestor's suggestions, Diomedes and Odysseus go to spy on the Trojan positions. They capture Dolon, an enemy scout, and using information they extract from him, kill the Thracian Rhesus and some of his men.

XI The next morning, fighting resumes. Several leading Achaeans are wounded, including Agamemnon (despite some valiant exploits), Diomedes and Odysseus; and led by Hector, the Trojans push the Achaeans back to their camp. Achilles, watching the retreat from his ship, sends Patroclus to find out about one of the casualties. Nestor appeals to Patroclus to rejoin the battle himself, even if Achilles still refuses to fight, and to wear Achilles' armour, so as to frighten the Trojans back.

XII Before Patroclus can return to Achilles, the Trojans attack the Achaean camp. Hector smashes open a gate in the Achaean wall, and the Trojans break through.

XIII The two armies fight on the beach, as the Trojans strive to reach the Achaean ships. In Zeus' absence, Poseidon encourages the Achaean resistance. Hector's advance is checked by Ajax.

XIV Hera seduces Zeus in a plan to distract his attention from the war. While he sleeps, Poseidon rouses the Achaeans, and the Trojans are driven back. Hector is stunned by Ajax.

XV When Zeus wakes, he makes Poseidon withdraw and has Hector restored by Apollo. With Hector at their head, the Trojans drive their opponents back to the ships once more, and try to set fire to them. Ajax leads the Achaean resistance.

XVI Patroclus returns to Achilles, who allows him to borrow his armour and lead out his men, but warns him against pursuing the Trojans too far. Hector at last drives Ajax back, and the first ship is set on fire; but on Patroclus' arrival, the Trojans are repulsed. Patroclus' victims include the Lycian Sarpedon, son of Zeus. Ignoring Achilles' warning, Patroclus drives the Trojans back to their city wall, and is confronted by Apollo himself, who stuns and disarms him. The Trojan Euphorbus wounds him, and Hector kills him.

XVII Hector takes Patroclus' armour, but the Achaeans, in retreat, succeed in reaching their camp with Patroclus' body. Menelaus and Ajax, Hector and Aeneas, distinguish themselves in the fighting.

XVIII Achilles hears of Patroclus' death with intense grief, and determines on revenge against Hector in battle. Thetis points out that his own death must follow Hector's, but promises that Hephaestus will make him new armour. Patroclus' body is brought to safety, and Hephaestus makes the new arms, including an elaborate shield.

XIX At Odysseus' instigation, Achilles agrees to a formal reconciliation with Agamemnon, and accepts his gifts. Achilles puts on his new armour, and Xanthus, his immortal horse, foretells his death.

XX Zeus in council gives the gods permission to take part in the fighting. As they descend to earth, Achilles begins a murderous assault on the Trojans. Those who face him are killed or escape only with divine assistance; Aeneas is rescued from him by Poseidon, Hector by Apollo. The Trojans retreat.

XXI The Trojan retreat is hampered by the river Scamander. Achilles fills the water with corpses, and the river, in protest, rises against him; but Hephaestus checks the water with his fire. Some of the Olympian gods now confront one another, and Athene strikes down Ares and Aphrodite. The gods return to Olympus, but outside Troy a trick by Apollo diverts Achilles, while the Trojans take refuge inside the city wall.

XXII Achilles hurries back and finds Hector alone outside the wall, prepared to meet him. As Achilles comes near, Hector takes to flight and, with Apollo's help, stays out of reach. Then Apollo leaves him and Athene induces him to stand and fight. In single combat Achilles kills Hector and fastens the body to his chariot. Dragging it behind him, he drives to the Achaean camp, while Hector's family watch in distress from Troy.

XXIII During the night Patroclus' ghost visits Achilles and asks for a swift burial. The next day his body is given a magnificent funeral. Afterwards the Achaeans hold athletic contests, at which Achilles presides.

XXIV After eleven days, Hector's body still lies unburied and defiled, although Apollo has kept it safe from permanent damage. The gods instruct Priam to bring Achilles a ransom for his son's body and Achilles to accept the ransom. By night, with the guidance of the god Hermes, Priam duly visits the Achaean camp and is treated with consideration by Achilles. Before daybreak he returns to Troy with Hector's body. The Trojan women, led by Andromache, make their laments over the body, and the poem ends with Hector's funeral.

13 Shape and structure

The *Iliad* has a central figure, Achilles, and the poem falls into three main sections, defined by Achilles' action or inaction: I–IX, consisting of the quarrel between Achilles and Agamemnon, the opening phase of battle, and the embassy to Achilles; X–XVII, the Trojan advance in the absence of Achilles, culminating in the death of Patroclus; XVIII–XXIV, the reappearance of Achilles, his combat with Hector, and his reconciliation with Priam. The sequence of these three parts and of the main events within them is lucid and coherent. However, this does not make the *Iliad* a tight 'organic' structure like (say) a Sophoclean tragedy, in which the action proceeds according to rigorous principles of causal logic. Aristotle, who first articulated the notion of organic structure, indeed saw Homer as a precursor of the Greek tragedians in that respect (*Poetics* viii), and a partial analysis of the poem in Aristotelian terms could be offered: (*a*) Achilles' withdrawal (I) results in (*b*) the gradual ascendancy of the Trojans (IV–XV), which prompts (*c*) first the unsuccessful embassy (IX) and then the intervention of Patroclus (XVI), whose death leads to (*d*) the re-entry of Achilles (XVIII–XX), whose inevitable consequence is (*e*) the killing of Hector and (granted the intensity of Achilles' feelings) the maltreatment of his corpse (XXII), a 'problem' which is resolved by (*f*) Priam's ransom (XXIV). In these terms, the contents of four books – I, IX, XVI, XXII – are pivotal. In I Achilles reacts appropriately to the wrong done him; in IX, inappropriately, he rejects a handsome attempt to put the wrong right and, by this obstinacy, propels his friend Patroclus to step into the breach; in XVI Patroclus is duly killed by Hector; in XXII Achilles kills Hector and so gives his dead friend his due. Of these books, XXII represents the climax of the poem, not only because it marks the culmination of Achilles' return to action and his revenge on Hector, but also because the killing of Hector ensures Achilles' own death in the imminent future, as is made clear to him by Thetis (XVIII 96).

More generally, we observe that like a Greek tragedy, and unlike (say) a Dickensian novel, the *Iliad* exhibits a strict unity of action in the sense that all the human material belongs to a single narrative thread: there are no sub-plots, although there is intermittent activity on the part of Zeus and the other gods. Furthermore, the action all takes place in one comprehensible location, the city and hinterland of Troy – except, again, for the divine action located on Mount Olympus. Then again, the action is relatively concentrated in time, with the main events, from the start of the fighting to the death of Hector, taking up a mere four days.

In Aristotelian terms, however, substantial parts of the poem are clearly tangential to the action. This might even be said of some of the material that involves the central figures, such as the rescue of Patroclus' body (XVII), or many of Achilles' exploits in XXI, or the games in XXIII. But above all, the long sequence of fighting, IV–XV, represents a series of events which are, to a large extent, sequential rather than consequential. Particular heroes have their particular hours of glory, the tide of battle ebbs and flows for both armies, various gods intervene at various moments – all with the result that, while some events follow earlier events 'by probability or necessity' (as Aristotle puts it), many others merely 'come next', as unpredictably as, indeed, the actual events of an inconclusive war might strike an eye-witness at the time.

The fact is that the poem, to a considerable extent, is organised on principles of a strictly non-Aristotelian kind. One of these is 'ringform'. The *Iliad*, as we have mentioned (p. 21), shows a degree of formal organisation independent of the logic of its contents, in a circular symmetry between beginning and end. It begins with a ransom and an argument (I), a ceremonial aggregation of forces (II), and a duel (III), and ends with a comparable sequence in reverse. Framed between this beginning and this end is a long sequence, largely consisting of fighting and less rigorously defined either by logical connections or by any formal symmetry. In this sense the poem is not simply tripartite, but presents, in effect, an $A - B - A$ shape. Overall, then, there is a marked contrast between (on the one hand) the sharply distinct and recurrent events of the opening and closing books and (on the other) the constantly shifting lights and shades of the battle sections. The effect – in musical, rather than pictorial, terms – is of a composition that moves from an implicit consonance into a protracted dissonance, and at last finds its 'inevitable', explicit, consonance again.

Another operative principle, wholly un-Aristotelian, is a tendency towards autonomy in some of the sections of the poem. Irrespective of their logical (or other) functions within the whole *Iliad*, the embassy to Achilles (IX) or the meeting of Achilles and Priam (XXIV) have a kind of self-sufficiency which makes it possible to read them as miniature wholes, as one cannot read a scene from a Sophoclean play. The separateness of X, the 'Doloneia' (pp. 7, 39), shows this tendency at its most extreme. Its external cause, no doubt, is the habits and expectations of ordinary oral performance, for which a scene of about a book's length is a natural unit. But there is also an aesthetic rationale: the development of *situation*. The embassy in IX provides a good example. It begins with the ambassadors making their way along the shore to Achilles' quarters. We watch them as they find him 'delighting his heart with his shrill lyre, fair and richly wrought, with a silver bridge on it', to which he 'sings' the 'glorious deeds of men' while Patroclus sits opposite him in silence (186ff.). Achilles is taken aback to see them, jumps up with the lyre still in his hand, and gives them hospitality (193ff.). After this striking tableau of action, we have an equally striking tableau of speech, as three very different members of the Achaean leadership – Odysseus, shrewdest of the heroes, Ajax, the strong man, and Phoenix, Achilles' old tutor – seek to persuade their greatest warrior to return to the war. The opening speeches, by Odysseus (225ff.) and Achilles (308ff.), represent a new stage in the action: the one proposes the compromise that would change the course of the war, the other contains the contemptuous response that ensures a different and delayed 'solution' to the crisis. The talking closes with a pair of short speeches from Ajax (624ff.) and Achilles (644ff.), but before these comes a long speech from Phoenix (434–605).

Phoenix is distressed. He feels a duty to stay with Achilles, but he is sure that Achilles' duty is to accept the new offer. He recalls the original instructions of Achilles' father, Peleus, to him, and how he came into Peleus' circle in the first place. Finally he offers Achilles a cautionary tale of the legendary hero Meleager which, like all the other pleas, fails to move him. Achilles' response (607ff.) is to offer Phoenix hospitality and a place of honour for the future – but reconciliation with Agamemnon he rejects as obstinately as before.

Before IX Phoenix plays no part in the *Iliad*, and he plays very little part in it thereafter: what his speech may tell us about himself, therefore, is neither here nor there. Nor does it affect Achilles' decision, which is already taken: it is, in any case, needlessly long for such a purpose. It does tell us something about Achilles in the past, and equally something about Achilles now, in that it serves to differentiate his current reaction to Agamemnon from his more amiable outlook as a whole; in particular, it sharpens the sense of a blind vendetta, of a wronged man now putting himself in the wrong. But what it does, beyond this and above all, is prolong and develop a moment of high emotion and significance, one which is marked off as special by its tense and vivid opening and is then articulated by the sequence of speeches for which Phoenix's provides a long, climactic crescendo.

The embassy is one of several dramatic personal confrontations in the poem, and each of them shows the same situational tendency. This is most obvious with the death-scenes of the major heroes – Sarpedon's and Patroclus' in XVI, Hector's in XXII. It is also true of the meetings between Priam and Helen on the walls of Troy (III), between Hector and his wife and child (VI), between Achilles and Priam (XXIV). In all such scenes the emotional moment tends to be both prolonged and articulated by speeches.

The *Iliad* makes use of an unexpected structural technique, which might be called *illusionist*. The first book directs us to the argument between Achilles and Agamemnon and its immediate consequences. There follows, in II, Agamemnon's dream, his proposal to the army, Thersites' bit of trouble-making, Odysseus' counteraction – and then, in the rest of II, the mobilisation and the catalogue of forces. Mobilisations and catalogues, however, are (on reflection) a surprising sequel to this series of events. They would most naturally arise in the first year of a war, not in the tenth. Without seeming grossly out of place, this section in fact evokes the beginning of the whole war. And in the books that follow, a remarkable series of events and depictions does the same.

In III the figures in the foreground are Helen, Paris and Menelaus: the triangle from which the war arose. At 166ff., for the benefit of her father-in-law Priam, Helen identifies the Achaean chieftains from the walls of Troy, as she would have had more reason to do in a year one than a year ten. After this comes a symbolic re-enactment of the original crime and *casus belli* in the duel between the original parties to the dispute, Paris and Menelaus. Menelaus is the rightful possessor of Helen and appropriately has the better of the duel (as Agamemnon protests, 457), but Paris is allowed to flout propriety. His sexuality charmed Helen away to Troy, and now he evades justice by sexual means: Aphrodite, the love-goddess, rescues him from defeat (374ff.), plants him in his bedroom (382), and has the guilty couple, Paris and Helen, make love (389–448) while Menelaus forlornly scours the battlefield and his brother vainly demands compensation (449–60).

The same original crime is evoked a second time in the next book (IV). A truce still holds between the two sides. The truce is broken by a single act of treachery that precipitates general fighting: a shot by the Trojan Pandarus at (appropriately) Menelaus (86ff.). Neither here nor in II–III is there any overt violation of the notional 'unity of time', but by a kind of illusion Homer offers us a series of events expressive of the span of the war from its cause to the impasse a decade later and, thereby, expressive of both the scale of the war and its moral contours.

At the same time, the *Iliad* evokes the war's end. 'The day will come', says Hector to Andromache (and likewise Agamemnon to

Menelaus), 'when sacred Ilios will be destroyed, and Priam, and the people of Priam' (VI 448–9, IV 164–5). The destruction of Troy is prefigured by Hector's death: he is Troy's protector (VI 403), and the city cannot survive without him. As Andromache foresees, her baby son will never live to manhood, because 'this city will be utterly destroyed first. For you have perished who watched over it' (XXIV 726ff.). Achilles' death, too, is prefigured by Hector's, as Thetis tells us (XVIII 96). Accordingly, when Priam makes the hazardous journey to Achilles' quarters to beg for Hector's body, it is almost as if this was already a journey to the land of the dead. His dear ones mourn for him 'as if for one going down to death' (XXIV 328). His guide is Hermes – Hermes who was also *psukhopompós*, conductor of souls. And Priam's innocent address to his killer-host has the impress of Achilles' impending death on it: 'Remember your father, Achilles . . . He too, it may be, is hard pressed by those around him, with no one to defend him from ruin. But at least he can hear that you are still alive, and be glad, and hope every day to see his son return from Troy. Whereas I . . .' (XXIV 486ff.) – whereas I, Priam, have lost my sons, and especially Hector, killed by you, Achilles. The implicit irony of the passage is crushing. By killing Priam's son, Achilles has in effect killed himself, so that Priam's analogy between himself and Achilles' father is more exact than he knows.

If, then, the duel between Menelaus and Paris in III evokes the source of the conflict, the matching duel of Hector and Achilles in XXII evokes its outcome. Furthermore, the very length and untidiness of the fighting in the books between these duels serves to give an illusion of the blur of ten years' conflict, even though, in truth, only a few days' fighting is directly represented there. The *Iliad*, therefore, presents a single phase and aspect of the Trojan war, one which is short enough and connected enough for 'organic' art, yet also such that it can be made to suggest a panorama of the war as a whole.

Another important principle underlies the organisation of the *Iliad*: parallelism. The poem involves series of heroes, combats, supplications, divine interventions, deaths, and so on. These are, by their very nature, series of parallel items; and it is clear that the parallels are often used to structural effect. Sometimes the effects involve links across the poem: we associate the items and note similarities – and differences – between them. A straightforward instance is the repeated phraseology used for the deaths of Patroclus and Hector (p. 15). Another is Andromache's three laments for Hector: VI 499, XXII 477ff., XXIV 725ff. Number one (only referred to) is the first lament anyone makes for Hector, made while he still lives, after his last meeting with his wife and son; number two is the last, and the chief, lament on his death; number three is the first, and again the chief, lament at his funeral. All three represent special moments in Hector's career.

In many cases we have an ascending series of parallel instances, where, in effect, the earlier prepare for the later. Various Achaean heroes have their hour of supremacy, their so-called *aristeia*, when no one on the battle-field can withstand them. Achilles' *aristeia* (XX–XXII) is the climactic instance of a series consisting of (most notably) Diomedes' (V), Agamemnon's (XI), and Patroclus' (XVI). Patroclus' *aristeia* inevitably offers a specific link with Achilles'. Patroclus is Achilles' close friend and almost his *alter ego*. He goes into battle as Achilles' surrogate in Achilles' armour and is at first taken for Achilles (XVI 278ff.), thereby vicariously fulfilling Achilles' promise to rejoin the fighting when the Trojans set fire to the Achaean fleet (IX 650ff.; XVI 80ff., 122ff., 284ff.). Again, Achilles' duel with Hector (XXII) is the climactic instance of a series involving Menelaus and Paris (III) and Ajax and Hector (VII). It is also the climactic instance of a series of combats within his own *aristeia*: he fights the Trojans *en masse* (XX), then the river Scamander (XXI), then Hector (XXII). Major is preceded by minor: the fight for Patroclus' body (XVII) by the fight for Sarpedon's (XVI 532–683). The great deaths of Sarpedon (XVI), Patroclus (XVI) and Hector (XXII) form an ascending series which is preceded by the deaths of countless lesser figures from IV onwards. The apparently inconsequential fighting which is transformed by the intervention of Patroclus precedes the fighting dominated by Achilles, the consequences of which are obvious to all. The first heroes to fight are the middle-rank warriors Paris and Menelaus (III); Hector does not take any proper part in the fighting until V (493ff.), Achilles not until XX.

Preparation can be used, more fundamentally, as a programmatic statement of a large theme to come. Book I begins with Apollo dishonoured and vengeful, then with the destruction he causes in his revenge and the settlement of his claim. This sequence – dishonour, revenge, destruction, settlement – prefigures the rhythm of the whole epic; and Achilles' own dishonouring and revenge follow (logically as well as sequentially) at once.

In some sequences, finally, contrast is seen to play a formative role, with or without some element of parallelism as well. A case in point is Patroclus' funeral and the games that follow it (XXIII). In these ritual manoeuvres we find a salutary contrast to the elementally physical intensity of XXII on one side and the moral intensity of XXIV on the other. The contrast is salutary for us, as readers, and for Achilles, as actor. In the games, in particular, Achilles is able to act as magnanimous master of ceremonies, awarding prizes and sorting out disputes in preparation for his role as magnanimous human being, dispensing human feeling to Priam, in the last book. Yet his reconciliation with Priam is itself as much a matter of ritual as of practical effect. Yes, Priam will get his son's body back; but no, the war will shortly be resumed (XXIV 665–70) – to the destruction of Priam and Achilles, among others.

As an organisational entity the *Iliad* has its limitations. In the first place, the predilection for situations and, perhaps, for contrasts produces some episodes which may be rich in colour and movement, but to the point where they become at odds with the poem as a whole. Thus: the Doloneia (X) offers a striking sequence of dramatic action, in marked contrast to all the talking in IX. But the Doloneia is not simply dramatic: it is melodramatic. It reveals the Achaeans as brave and resourceful, as they have to be after the failure of the embassy, but by means of a surprise nocturnal raid which makes the Trojans seem inept. Such melodramatic extremes, however, and, above all, such a prejudicial view of the Trojans, are hardly in evidence elsewhere. Again: the *Iliad* assumes both the pettiness and the huge power of the gods, but the battle of the Olympians (the 'theomachy') in XXI develops these premises to a point which struck one ancient critic as blasphemous ('Longinus', *On the Sublime*, ix 6–8), and which is certainly of questionable propriety within the poem's own terms.

More important, it is difficult not to feel that the long sequence of fighting books in the middle of the *Iliad* is too long – not in any one part, but simply too long overall: its elaboration is insufficiently decisive – or incisive. The point is that the logic of parallelism in these books, and especially the multiplication of ascending series, has produced a massive sequence of movements and confrontations, advances and retreats, storms and lulls, whose individual necessity is rarely demonstrable. There is in fact an insoluble problem here, for the protracted and (more or less) undifferentiated mass of fighting is needed *cumulatively*, both to prepare for the return of Achilles and – by illusionist logic – to provide a sense of the scale and scope of the whole protracted war. The *Iliad* demands the mass of fighting, but does not demand its particular details. Rather, the opening of the poem sets up 'Aristotelian' expectations of strict causal logic (reinforced by the close of the poem), for which the middle provides no adequate satisfaction nor any adequate substitute. The lucidity, subtlety and coherence of the *Iliad* are remarkable; the constructional problem represented by its central books is its most serious limitation.

14 Translation

Turning from the *Iliad's* structure to the linguistic particulars on which its vitality depends, most modern readers will at once be faced with the problem of translation. All translation of poetry is problematic, because of the way that poetry tends to capitalise on, and explore, distinctive features of its own language and to produce, in consequence, a dense texture of meaning dependent on particular words in a particular order. The translator of (let us say) Shakespeare is wont to replace this kind of density with a simpler comprehensible outline – or else the exploratory with the merely exotic.

The main difficulty confronting the translator of Homer is different. To a modern eye, or ear, Homeric poetry is not especially dense, but it is cast in an alien idiom. In the first place, Homer's is a strangely composite dialect, with its archaisms and alternative forms, and a strangely conventional phraseology, with all its recurrent elements. At the same time, the actual vocabulary of this poetic language is strange in another way: it is predominantly concrete, vastly more so than the vocabulary of any modern poetry is likely to be, because it presupposes a phase of speech prior to the great development of

Western abstract thought and expression from fifth-century Greece
to our own scientific era. The net result is that any attempt to render
Homer by the obvious equivalents of a modern language is liable to
produce a wholly different effect – and often very little effect at all –
whereas any attempt to produce the effect may have to make use of
quite different linguistic mechanisms. Hence a 'literal' translation
of Homer is as inadequate and misleading as a literal translation of
Shakespeare, after all.

In practice, different translations of the *Iliad* have different ade-
quacies and inadequacies. Here is a representative passage from the
fighting books, XVI 342–57, first in Homer's Greek:

> Mēriónēs d' Akámanta kikheìs posì karpalímoisi
> núx' híppōn epibēsómenon katà dexiòn ômon:
> ḗripe d' ex okhéōn, katà d' ophthalmôn kékhut' akhlús.
> Idomeneùs d' Erúmanta katà stóma nēléï khalkôi
> núxe: tò d' antikrù dóru khálkeon exepérēse
> nérthen hup' enkepháloio, kéasse d' ár' ostéa leuká:
> ek dè tínakhthen odóntes, enéplēsthen dé hoi ámphō
> haímatos ophthalmoí: tò d' anà stóma kaì katà rhînas
> prêse khanốn: thanátou dè mélan néphos amphekálupsen.
> hoûtoi ár' hēgemónes Danaôn hélon ándra hékastos.
> hōs dè lúkoi árnessin epékhraon ề eríphoisi
> síntai, hupèk mḗlōn haireúmenoi, hai t' en oressi
> poiménos aphradíēisi diétmagen: hoi dè idóntes
> aîpsa diharpázousin análkida thumòn ekhoúsas:
> hōs Danaoì Trṓessin epékhraon: hoi dè phóboio
> duskeládou mnḗsanto, láthonto dè thoúridos alkês.

Now in a verse translation by Robert Fitzgerald (1974):

> Meriones on the run overtook Acamas
> mounting behind his horses and hit his shoulder,
> knocking him from the car. Mist swathed his eyes.
> Idomeneus thrust hard at Erymas' mouth
> with his hard bronze. The spearhead passed on through
> beneath his brain and split the white brain-pan.
> His teeth were dashed out, blood filled both his eyes,
> and from his mouth and nostrils as he gaped
> he spurted blood. Death's cloud enveloped him.
> There each Danaan captain killed his man.

As ravenous wolves come down on lambs and kids
astray from some flock that in hilly country
splits in two by a shepherd's negligence,
and quickly wolves bear off the defenceless things,
so when Danaans fell on Trojans, shrieking
flight was all they thought of, not of combat.

Now in a prose version by Andrew Lang, Walter Leaf and Ernest Myers (1892):

Now Meriones overtook Akamas with swift strides, and smote him on the right shoulder, as he went up into his chariot, and he slipped out of his chariot, and mist was poured over his eyes. And Idomeneus wounded Erymas on the mouth with the pitiless bronze, and the spear of bronze went clean through below, beneath the brain, and shattered his white bones, and his teeth were shaken out, and both his eyes were filled with blood, and he blew blood up through mouth and nostrils as he gaped, and the black cloud of death covered him about.

Thus those leaders of the Danaans slew each his man. But even as robber wolves fall on the lambs or kids, choosing them out of the herds, when they are scattered on hills by the witlessness of the shepherd, and the wolves behold it, and speedily harry the younglings that have no heart of courage, – even so the Danaans fell on the Trojans, and they were mindful of ill-sounding flight, and forgot their impetuous valour.

And finally in Alexander Pope's heroic couplets (1718):

O'ertaken *Neamas* by *Merion* bleeds;
Pierc'd thro' the Shoulder as he mounts his Steeds;
Back from the Car he tumbles to the Ground;
His swimming Eyes eternal Shades surround.
    Next *Erymas* was doom'd his Fate to feel,
His open'd Mouth receiv'd the *Cretan* Steel:
Beneath the Brain the Point a Passage tore,
Crash'd the thin Bones, and drown'd the Teeth in Gore:
His Mouth, his Eyes, his Nostrils pour a Flood;
He sobs his Soul out in the Gush of Blood.
    As when the Flocks, neglected by the Swain
(Or Kids, or Lambs) lie scatter'd o'er the Plain,
A Troop of Wolves th' unguarded Charge survey,
And rend the trembling, unresisting Prey.
Thus on the Foe the *Greeks* impetuous came;
Troy fled, unmindful of her former Fame.

From Pope, with his consistent Augustan idiom, the reader might gather that Homer was a substantial poet, though hardly of what sort. Lang, Leaf and Myers serve to suggest that the original is special: archaic, perhaps in some way biblical – and biblical narrative, with its authority and its distance from the reader, is not the worst analogy one might offer to the narrative of the *Iliad*. In Fitzgerald (as also in Lang, Leaf and Myers) the reader might sense the clear concreteness of the Greek, whereas Pope introduces various emotive semi-abstractions: *white* bones (*ostéa leuká*) become 'thin' bones (human fragility and all that); Erymas, *blowing* or *puffing* his blood up (*prêse*) with his *mouth open* (*khanôn*), instead 'sobs his soul out in the gush' of blood. Fitzgerald also conveys the impression of action more urgently than the others – if anything, too urgently. In terms of 'literal' equivalence to the original, Lang, Leaf and Myers' version is much the closest, Pope's much the furthest away.

More important: the distinction of Homer's poetry is lost both by Fitzgerald with his half-prosaic verse and by Lang, Leaf and Myers with their archaising prose. Fitzgerald's version is not as dated as theirs, but it has less dignity, partly because it lacks the assurance of a consistent idiom. '[Flight] was all they thought of' is ordinary modern speech; 'ravenous wolves' belongs to olde worlde fairy tales or romantic ballads; 'shrieking flight', with its harsh transference, is a not very felicitous attempt at a twentieth-century poeticism; '[shepherd's] negligence' suggests a law report; 'brain-pan' is what Matthew Arnold, in a famous discussion (*On Translating Homer*, 1861), would have stigmatised as 'quaint'. It is not so much that none of these phrases has a Homeric effect, but that each one is un-Homeric in a different way. 'Passed on through beneath' reveals a translator's anxiety to be 'faithful', at whatever cost to the English. 'Mist *swathed* his eyes' (like a bandage? – the Greek is closer to Lang, Leaf and Myers' 'was poured over'): this chunky expression betrays, on the other side, an underlying sense of the incapacity of prosaic verse to convey Homer's tone and impact and a desire to compensate. Though not indeed conveyed by Lang, Leaf and Myers either, that tone and impact is at least inferential (so to speak) from the faint biblical resonance of their unpretentious catalogue: 'and his teeth were shaken out, and both his eyes were filled with blood, and . . . and . . . .'. Their weakest points are precisely their lapses from the quasi-biblical norm ('mindful of ill-sounding flight').

Pope's couplets do, however, exercise a true literary effect. 'A pretty poem, Mr Pope, but you must not call it Homer', a contemporary scholar, Richard Bentley, is alleged to have said; and it is easy to see that Pope's effect relies heavily on the obliteration of much Homeric detail (including, accidentally, the name *Akámas*) and the incorporation of much that is non-Homeric. The new detail is partly baroque emotionalism ('bleeds', 'feel', 'thin', 'sobs . . . out', 'soul', 'trembling'), partly neo-classical rhetoric: here belong the conventional figures of speech ('Troy fled') and the pervasive balance and contrast that Pope's couplets so readily accommodate. The rise to the climactic antithesis, '. . . the Greeks impetuous came; / Troy fled . . .', is characteristic.

Pope's overall effect is indeed different from Homer's: Homer becomes an Augustan. Yet the strength represented by Pope's Augustanism, though not Homeric and too narrow to be Homeric, is a strength beyond anything available to the two contrasting 'modern' translations. It would seem that the idioms at their disposal are less suitable *even* than his to do the job. And this would still be the case if Fitzgerald ('shepherd's negligence') eliminated his particular infelicities and Lang, Leaf and Myers ('mindful of ill-sounding flight') eliminated theirs.

The point may be made more conclusively by a second comparison between the same three translations. The passage this time involves a speech, the splendid speech by Sarpedon in which he urges his friend Glaucus to join him in an assault on the Achaean wall (XII 307–28). Fitzgerald:

> So valour drove
> Sarpedon to the wall to make a breakthrough.
>   Turning to Glaucus, Hippolochus' son, he said:
> 'What is the point of being honoured so
> with precedence at table, choice of meat,
> and brimming cups, at home in Lycia,
> like gods at ease in everyone's regard?
> And why have lands been granted you and me
> on Xanthus bank: to each his own demesne,
> with vines and fields of grain?
>   'So that we two
> at times like this in the Lycian front line

may face the blaze of battle and fight well,
that Lycian men-at-arms may say:
"They are no common men, our lords who rule
in Lycia. They eat fat lamb at feasts
and drink rare vintages, but the main thing is
their fighting power, when they lead in combat!"
    'Ah, cousin, could we but survive this war
to live forever deathless, without age,
I would not ever go again to battle,
nor would I send you there for honour's sake!
But now a thousand shapes of death surround us,
and no man can escape them, or be safe.
Let us attack – whether to give some fellow
glory or to win it from him.'

Lang, Leaf and Myers:

So did his heart then urge on the godlike Sarpedon to rush against
the wall, and break through the battlements. And instantly he spake
to Glaukos, son of Hippolochos: 'Glaukos, wherefore have we twain the
chiefest honour, – seats of honour, and messes, and full cups in Lykia, and
all men look on us as gods? And wherefore hold we a great demesne by the
banks of Xanthos, a fair demesne of orchard-land, and wheat-bearing
tilth? Therefore now it behoveth us to take our stand in the first rank of
the Lykians, and encounter fiery battle, that certain of the well-corsleted
Lykians may say, "Verily our kings that rule Lykia be no inglorious men,
they that eat fat sheep, and drink the choice wine honey-sweet: nay, but
they are also of excellent might, for they war in the foremost ranks of the
Lykians." Ah, friend, if once escaped from this battle we were for ever
to be ageless and immortal, neither would I fight myself in the foremost
ranks, nor would I send thee into the war that giveth men renown, but
now – for assuredly ten thousand fates of death do every way beset us,
and these no mortal may escape nor avoid – now let us go forward,
whether we shall give glory to other men, or others to us.'

And Pope:

    Resolv'd alike, divine *Sarpedon* glows
With gen'rous Rage that drives him on the Foes.
He views the Tow'rs, and meditates their Fall,
To sure Destruction dooms th' aspiring Wall;
Then casting on his Friend an ardent Look,

Fir'd with the Thirst of Glory, thus he spoke.
      Why boast we, *Glaucus!* our extended Reign,
Where *Xanthus'* Streams enrich the *Lycian* Plain,
Our num'rous Herds that range the fruitful Field,
And Hills where Vines their purple Harvest yield,
Our foaming Bowls with purer Nectar crown'd,
Our Feasts enhanc'd with Music's sprightly Sound?
Why on those Shores are we with Joy survey'd,
Admir'd as Heroes, and as Gods obey'd?
Unless great Acts superior Merit prove,
And vindicate the bount'ous Pow'rs above.
'Tis ours, the Dignity they give, to grace;
The first in Valour, as the first in Place.
That when with wond'ring Eyes our martial Bands
Behold our Deeds transcending our Commands,
Such, they may cry, deserve the sov'reign State,
Whom those that envy, dare not imitate!
Could all our Care elude the gloomy Grave,
Which claims no less the fearful than the brave,
For Lust of Fame I should not vainly dare
In fighting Fields, nor urge thy Soul to War.
But since, alas! ignoble Age must come,
Disease, and Death's inexorable Doom;
The Life which others pay, let us bestow,
And give to Fame what we to Nature owe;
Brave tho' we fall, and honour'd if we live,
Or let us Glory gain, or Glory give!

The Sarpedon passage is appreciably more intense than the fighting narrative, and the intensity accentuates the problem that the 'modern' translators face. Under the strain, Lang, Leaf and Myers' archaism sinks from the timeless biblical to the clumsy mock-Tudor; and if 'twain' and 'behoveth' are disconcerting in their distance from acceptable literary idiom, 'wherefore . . . wherefore . . . therefore' is so distracting as almost to obscure the plain meaning. Under the same strain, Fitzgerald's attempt at an attenuated verse language breaks down more comprehensively. Our sensibilities are assailed by an unresolved and utterly un-Homeric alternation of idioms between the prosaic and the melodramatic, with 'turning to', 'the main thing is' and 'some fellow' at one extreme and 'forever deathless'

and 'a thousand shapes of death' at the other. Symptomati-
cally, Fitzgerald is unhappy with Homer's generic epithets: godlike
Sarpedon loses his and the well-corsleted Lycians theirs. We may
note that direct speech – both in Homer and in general – is more given
to emotional intensity than narrative; that the lack of a standard
idiom is particularly marked in twentieth-century (English) speech;
and that twentieth-century (English) poetry is less given to emotional intensity than to irony and understatement. By way of cor-
roborating the point, we may add that when Homer is less intense,
Fitzgerald can be very much more successful (see pp. 60, 99).

In contrast to later translators, Pope revels in the passage; and
his whole-hearted yet urbane rendering certainly provides a closer
equivalent to the tone, the rhythm and the quality of the Greek. Yet
that equivalence is bought at a high cost: dozens of un-Homeric
points of detail, an expansion of the passage by about half, and a
recasting of its material, whereby, representatively, fat sheep and
honey-sweet wine move up a few sentences (to become 'numerous
herds' and 'bowls with nectar crowned'). It is understandable that
Bentley's refusal to 'call it Homer' should have been echoed by many
Homeric scholars from his day to our own.

None of this sounds very consoling to readers of the *Iliad* in translation, especially readers who have no corrective access to the Greek.
And it has to be added that direct speech, where modern versions are
likely to be least adequate, makes up almost half of the whole epic.
But forewarned is forearmed. A judicious reading of (or, at least, alternation between) different translations may give a very adequate
impression of their common target; and even the reader of any one
translation, if aware of the problems involved, will learn a good deal
about the poetic qualities of the original. And mercifully, some of the
mechanisms of those qualities are much less resistant to translation
than others.

15 Stylisation and immediacy

How are we to characterise the poetry of the *Iliad*? In *On Translating
Homer* Matthew Arnold offered one answer: Homer, he suggested,
was 'rapid' in movement, 'plain and direct' in syntax, phraseology
and ideas (Arnold called them 'evolution of thought', 'expression of

thought' and 'substance of thought'), and 'noble' in manner. This is certainly a recognisable description of the specimens of the *Iliad* that we have been looking at, and it would be easy to do as Arnold himself does, and criticise translators with reference to his formula: Fitzgerald lacks Homer's 'nobility', Pope (with his rhyming couplets) the 'rapid movement', and so on. On a broader front, one might say that Arnold's formula is both coherent and balanced, and serves to differentiate the *Iliad* from (say) Shakespeare or Sophocles or Virgil or Milton (let alone twentieth-century poetry), none of which are consistently 'rapid' or 'plain and direct' as Homer is. On the other hand, it does little or nothing to differentiate the *Iliad* from some minor post-Homeric verse, like early Greek elegy, or, for instance, from the prose of the New Testament Gospel narratives.

How shall we improve on Arnold's description? By concentrating, I suggest, on two central but contrasting qualities of the *Iliad*: immediacy (which Arnold refers to, in part, under the heading of 'plain and direct') and stylisation (which his formula neglects altogether, except insofar as 'noble' implies it).

Shakespearean verse has great immediacy, but immediacy associated with intensification of ordinary usage – 'the current language heightened', in Gerard Manley Hopkins' phrase: 'Light thickens, and the crow / Makes wing to the rooky wood'; 'Thou' lt come no more, / Never, never, never, never, never. / Pray you, undo this button'; 'To be imprisoned in the viewless winds, / And blown with restless violence.' Since Wordsworth's proclamation on behalf of 'the language really used by men' (Preface to *Lyrical Ballads*, 1802), we tend to assume that language that is to embody experience, convey it directly to us and affect us with it, will be basically language of this kind, however heightened it may be. Conversely (we expect), stylised expression, where words are organised into schematic patterns or conventional elements, over and above the conventions of ordinary speech – such expression interposes a barrier between us and experience which ensures that little or no immediacy is possible. This is a deficiency we tend to find in rhetorical literature. It is also a deficiency that many readers (like Wordsworth) tend to find in neo-classical poetry, even poetry as distinguished as Pope's.

The verse of the *Iliad* is not like Shakespeare's any more than it is like Pope's. It is not consistently heightened, but it is very stylised *and yet* very immediate. Shakespearean immediacy works partly through the evocation of particulars (*light thickens*, as T. S. Eliot put it, 'conveys the feeling of being in a particular place at a particular time'). Homeric expression is different, most obviously because of its formulaic basis. The *Iliad*, we should recall, is not all equally formulaic (pp. 19ff.). Narrative is more formulaic than speech, ends of verses more than middles of verses, common subjects (like combats) more than less common subjects, minor combats more than major combats. Formulaic stylisation, accordingly, is much more apparent at some times than at others. Nevertheless, it remains a pervasive feature of Homer's poetry, and one of its invariable effects is to alert its audience not to the particular, but to the general.

As often, the noun-epithet groups offer convenient examples. An epithet in such groups is usually a generic epithet, whose propriety is independent of particular contexts, although a particular context may in fact evoke its propriety with particular force (p. 58). Achilles is *podárkēs dîos*, 'fleet-footed, great', at I 121, not because he is displaying either of those properties at that moment, but because those are among his prominent characteristics overall (p. 16). Such usage finds parallels in ordinary speech. We speak of 'a fast car', whether the car is in fact moving fast, moving slowly, or standing still. Nevertheless, the use of these epithets for Achilles is plainly a stylised one, as is their alternation with other epithets or with none at all.

It is a further stylisation that such epithets tend to be laudatory or neutral, but not pejorative. Achilles is 'great' and 'fleet-footed'. He is also hot-tempered and obstinate, but no such generic epithets are applied to him. And this is not simply a matter of heroising the heroes. Man-made artefacts, for instance, are treated similarly. Ships may be 'swift' (*thoaí*) or 'balanced' (*eîsai*): they are not frail or dangerous. Such a stylisation implies a distinctive perception of reality. Experience is seen as a ritual and, up to a point, a glorious ritual. More fundamentally still, the stylisation evokes the continuity and permanence of experience. A ship is a ship. It has a ship's proper qualities, which no temporary accident can affect. This ship's qualities are and remain every ship's qualities, just as Achilles now and Achilles then are, on the face of it, one and the same Achilles. 'The province of poetry', declared Samuel Johnson (*Rasselas*, 1759), 'is to describe nature and passion, which are always the same'. The poetry of the *Iliad* asserts the *dictum* in a special sense, widening the reference of 'nature' to include the 'natural' works and activities of man. This is sometimes true of quite elaborate human events. Hence we find 'different' meals described in identical fashion and messages transmitted in precisely their original form.

But stylisation pervades the poem on other levels too, notably in the stereotyping of scenes. This is most easily demonstrable with the combats. For a start, fighting is so presented as to exclude much that happens in life. In the *Iliad* warriors win by superior valour or might: there is next to no technique or strategy. They kill or are killed, but contrary to ordinary experience they are not taken prisoner, and they are rarely wounded seriously – or if they are, the wounds rarely disable their owners for long. At one point, as Patroclus reports to Achilles, chieftains of the calibre of Diomedes, Odysseus and Agamemnon are *hors de combat* (XVI 25–6); but neither they nor any other heroes ever have to be invalided out of the fighting for good. The descriptions of Meriones killing Acamas and Idomeneus killing Erymas (pp. 41ff.) may seem like individualised descriptions, but in fact they belong to related types, which begin with the point of impact ('the right shoulder', 'the mouth') and end with a conventional periphrasis for death ('mist spread over his eyes', 'death's black cloud covered him'). The major combats have their own stylised elements – not least the death-speeches that, by convention, the great are privileged to make 'even though their strength is spent'. This ritual honour (which survives into our own age in opera and the cinema) is granted to Sarpedon (XVI 492ff.), to Patroclus shortly afterwards (XVI 844ff.), and inevitably to Hector, whose special death is specially marked with a double death-speech (XXII 338ff., 356ff.).

In his distinguished book *Mimesis*, Erich Auerbach argued that Homeric poetry represents one main type of realism, projecting external reality and bringing to it a 'uniform illumination'. If, once again, we think of Meriones hitting Acamas on the right shoulder, or of Erymas puffing out blood through his mouth and nostrils, it is hard to disagree. Yet these remain stylised descriptions, and so, in one way or another, are most of the 'realistic' descriptions in the *Iliad*. Take the physical setting of the war. The fighting takes place mostly on a plain between the Achaean ships, drawn up on the shore, and the walled city of Troy. These bold and bare outlines are regularly referred to. Particular encounters, like Meriones' with Acamas and Idomeneus' with Erymas, happen somewhere within them, but their particular locations are rarely specified. This presentation of 'realistic' action in such a notional setting shows that *uniform* illumination is not the goal. The depiction of larger movements on the battlefield shows it more clearly still. These tend not to derive from external factors – like time or weather or terrain or any material reality – but from acts of will on the part of a hero or the god propelling him. 'And now to Tydeus' son, Diomedes, Pallas Athene gave might and courage . . . and she sent him charging down the middle, into the thick of the turmoil' (V 1ff.): external points of reference are entirely lacking, and even the propulsion 'down the middle' is as much a matter of Diomedes' newly found status – his centrality to the action – as of any spatial relationships.

In the context of Homeric stylisation, one phenomenon deserves special attention: the epic or 'extended' simile. 'Thus' – in Lang, Leaf and Myers' version – 'those leaders of the Danaans slew each his man. But even as robber wolves fall on the lambs or kids, choosing them out of the herds, when they are scattered on hills by the witlessness of the shepherd, and the wolves behold it, and speedily harry the younglings that have no heart of courage – even so the Danaans fell on the Trojans . . .' (XVI 351ff.; p. 42). This is one of some two hundred 'extended' similes, which constitute much the most obvious type of imagery in the poem. Metaphor (the most discussed type of poetic imagery) is associated with heightened, rather than stylised, usage. Accordingly, its great master among the greatest writers is Shakespeare – 'light thickens' – and accordingly, metaphor is largely absent from the *Iliad*. Short similes and comparisons do occur in the poem, but so they do in all poetry and even in colloquial language ('went like a bomb', 'good as gold'). The extended simile is special, and its frequency in the *Iliad* is unique in Greek literature and, probably, anywhere.

The name, 'extended simile', is a misnomer. It implies that the long epic simile is really an ordinary short one with an extension – as if our example ran, 'they fell on the Trojans like robber wolves, *which* . . .' Whatever the origin of the type, aesthetically this is false.

The long epic simile is a quite separate entity with its own special, and stylised, form: 'Even as . . ., which . . . – even so . . .' With an almost mathematical preciseness, the two terms of the comparison – the proper subject (or 'tenor') and the new material (or 'vehicle') – are set out side by side as equivalents, irrespective of the nature or the scope of what they have in common. Like the wolves-simile, most of the two hundred occur in the narrative, most of their vehicles belong to the world of nature, most of their tenors are human actions or moments belonging to human activity. The Danaans are not like wolves: the Danaans in action are like wolves in action.

There is a widespread belief (which again the name 'extended simile' tends to support) that the common element between the tenor and the vehicle of these similes is a 'point of comparison', usually initial, after which the vehicle is elaborated, like a digression, for its own sake. This is rarely the case. Often the allegedly singular 'point' is plural, as in the wolves-simile: the Danaans are like killer animals; the Trojans are like their victims; the Trojans, like the 'lambs or kids', are weaker and unable to resist or escape; the one assault is like the other assault. Furthermore, in this instance and in general, the characteristic focus on an action means that we respond not to specifiable points of comparison, single or multiple, but to an overall equivalence. Yes, the vehicle acquires a kind of self-sufficiency; it lives in its own right, it stands as a coherent image (in the true sense of the word). But no, this does not make any part of it a digression (in the true sense), because the coherent whole resists partition, and because without its coherence it could not be a self-sufficient image. Like a metaphor, then, but unlike the familiar short comparison, the epic simile is both solid and transparent: it exists in its own right, yet we also see through it.

In most of these similes (in the wolves-simile, for instance), the equivalence between tenor and vehicle is largely diagrammatic: the various points of correspondence produce the effect of an explanatory figure. This is normal, but not invariable. Sometimes the equivalence is impressionistic. A startling example is XVI 294ff.:

And the ship was left there half-burnt, but the Trojans were driven in flight with an awesome din, and the Danaans poured in among the ships, and the din became intense. And as when Zeus, rouser of lightning,

moves a thick cloud away from a great mountain's high peak, and all the
look-out spots come into view, and the tops of headlands, and valleys,
and the infinite air bursts open from the heavens – even so the Danaans
thrust destructive fire back from their ships and gained a short breathing-
space.

Here mood – in the vehicle, the implicitly welcoming mood of an
unmentioned onlooker – becomes a more important element in the
equivalence than the given material correspondence, *A* moves *B*
away from *C*.

And sometimes, more remarkably still, the equivalence itself is
subordinate to a quite different function. By virtue of its structure,
the epic simile tends to hold the narrative in suspended animation
at a certain moment, to evoke an equivalent to that moment, and
thereby to draw attention to it. And so distinctive are the similes,
so prominent in context, that their powers of drawing and holding
attention are very great, and their prominence comes to be exploited
as a potentiality of the image in its own right. Hence it arises that
similes are used not only to illustrate or interpret the moment of
action, but to signal its importance. The presence of the simile marks
the context as special, perhaps as a climax or a turning-point in the
action overall. In this way the impressionistic cloud-simile marks the
pregnant moment when Patroclus intervenes to save the Achaean
ships. The length of the vehicle may imply extra importance. The
Iliad contains many lion-similes, in most of which the vehicle is
a few verses long: the longest marks Achilles' return to battle (XX
164–73). And some very special moments attract clusters of similes;
above all, the moment when the Achaean forces, in all their magnificence, mobilise for action attracts no fewer than five long and four
short similes (II 455–83). The simile thus acquires an architectonic
function.

The epic simile, then, is a stylised element in the poem – and yet
it is also a source of quite various effects and, in its essential mode of
operation, even comparable with that prime source of immediacy,
metaphor. In the representative wolves-simile we do in fact seem to
apprehend the wolves themselves immediately and thereby apprehend the leaders of the Danaans, to whom they are compared, with
a double force, as we might in a metaphor. And in this the simile

is truly representative of Homeric poetry as a whole. For despite its pervasive stylisation, the poem has an extraordinary immediacy all its own.

The immediacy that we find in the *Iliad* depends on a number of seemingly distinct features of Homeric poetry, some of them features that Matthew Arnold discussed under the headings of 'rapidity', 'plainness', and 'directness'. In the first place, Homer's vocabulary, as we have pointed out (pp. 40f.), is considerably more concrete than any we normally encounter in the literature of later ages. This is as true of the most obviously formulaic elements as of any others. At XVI 347 Erymas' shattered bones, *ostéa*, are white, *leuká*, because Homeric *ostéa* are habitually *leuká*; but the simple collocation has a concrete force which its familiarity does not nullify.

Then again, Homeric word-order is relatively free (unlike the word-order of English and other modern European languages), yet not intricate (unlike Latin). Phrases and clauses are lucid on first hearing, with words that belong grammatically together (like adjectives and nouns) physically close together, as a word-by-word translation serves to show (e.g.):

> Meriones [*subject*] Acamas having-got <with> feet swift
> Hit, <as he was> <his> horses mounting, on <the> right shoulder:
> <He> crashed-down from <the> chariot; over <his> eyes spread mist.
> Idomeneus [*subject*] Erymas on <the> mouth <with> pitiless bronze
> Hit . . .   (XVI 342–6)

(where pointed brackets enclose words which Greek idiom leaves inexplicit). As the same example shows, Homeric syntax also tends to be simple and unconstricting: co-ordination is common, subordination limited. Metre too is hardly felt as a constraint. Flexible word-order, the formulaic system, and the range of alternatives within the linguistic composite (p. 23) combine – in creative hands – to make metre and sense work as one. In one respect, indeed, sense-rhythms are allowed to dominate. Enjambement is common (p. 13) and, furthermore, is often used to confer a special, sensuous immediacy on the context, as it is with the physical 'hits' (*núx'*, 343; *núxe*, 346) in the passage just quoted.

An important factor in Homer's immediacy is his freedom to call a spade a spade. His speakers tend to talk directly from their situation, as Sarpedon does to Glaucus (pp. 44ff.); and plain speaking certainly commends itself to Achilles ('I must have my say outright . . . Hateful as the gates of Hell is the man who has one thing hidden in his mind and says another', IX 309ff.). Again, while Homer's language is a largely archaic composite, his vocabulary is not a conventional poetic diction in the restrictive sense that Virgil's is, or Milton's, let alone Racine's. Some bodily functions, some types of physical unpleasantness, are left to be imagined, but in general few words or thoughts seem to be regarded as taboo. When Erymas is puffing out his blood, the unpleasantness of the moment is not exploited sadistically, but neither is it evaded squeamishly. Sex is treated in the same direct way: 'And Zeus, rouser of clouds, saw her [Hera]. And when he saw her, desire [*érōs*] spread over his heart, as it had done the first time they coupled in love [*emisgésthēn philótēti*], when the two of them went to bed [*eis eunèn phoitônte*] without the knowledge of their parents' (XIV 293ff.) – where the word for 'coupled' (*mísgesthai: mígnusthai*) is a normal Greek word regularly so used of animals, as well as men, from early epics to the biological treatises of Aristotle in the fourth century. As a regular act, sex is regularly described in these phrases. The description, therefore, is stylised, but the phraseology itself, and 'coupled' above all, is as direct as it could be.

A corollary of this kind of frankness is that heroic endeavour is described forcefully and without inhibition, even if that means presenting the grand in terms of the everyday or the low. Homer, that is, shares with Shakespeare ('undo this button') an absence of what more fastidious neo-classical ages – and many later epic poets – were to see as essential *decorum*. (Arnold's view of Homer as 'noble' is peculiarly misleading here.) This is most obvious in the similes, where, it seems, any and all experience is available for comparative purposes. Beside the 'heroic' comparisons of Achilles to a lion and the Achaeans to wolves, we have the men fighting over Sarpedon's body compared to flies on a farm, 'buzzing round the milk churns' (XVI 641 ff.), an arrow glancing off Menelaus' breastplate to beans bouncing off a shovel (XIII 586ff.), Scamander's boiling streams to the boiling water used for melting pig's fat (XXI 362ff.), Ajax, under pressure, to a donkey assailed by boys with sticks (XI 556ff.). The heroic world is enhanced, not diminished, by this relish for the variety of life.

Homer's frankness, directness, concreteness, help create a solid poetic reality, a reality not (in Auerbach's words) 'uniformly illuminated', but unquestionably a reality which is (as Auerbach suggested) primarily presented in terms of its outer surface. Everywhere in the *Iliad* we are struck by the external clarity and definition of events and things, of gods and men, of their responses and their recollections. We find this with Sarpedon, articulating his situation, step by step, to his friend Glaucus; with Erymas, puffing out his blood (a wholly external physical action anyway, we would say); with Athene, rushing Diomedes into the thick of the fighting (partly an externalisation of an act of a man's will, we might say).

The representation of the gods requires discussion in its own right (pp. 69ff.). It has a special significance here in that its definiteness and detail ensure that no realm of the unknown or unknowable exists to cast doubt on the solidity of the human and material world. There is one exception to this: the vagueness with which ultimate causality is presented. I apologise, says Agamemnon, but I am not to blame: no, 'it was Zeus and Fate and the avenging Fury that walks in the mist [*ēerophoîtis*]' (XIX 87). Zeus, like the rest of the Greek pantheon, is presented with a marvellous clarity in the *Iliad*; the avenging Fury (*Erinús*), despite her vivid epithet, is little more than a name; and Fate (*Moîra*) is an obscure entity, whose status and whose relationships to us and the gods are never made clear. At one moment we seem to find Zeus (and the other gods?) presented as the symbol of Fate, as when he holds up his gold scales, weighs the fates of Hector and Achilles, and finds the fate of Hector heavier in the scale – 'and Phoebus Apollo', who had sustained Hector up to that moment, 'left him' (XXII 213). At another moment Zeus can resent the course of Fate and even entertain thoughts of overruling Fate, as he does before Hector's death (XXII 174ff.). But such uncertainties are few. In general, the poem fills us with the sense of direct, lucid, present experience – for all that the 'presence' is substantially that of a lost and irrecoverable legendary world.

The immediacy and the stylisation of Homeric poetry do not simply co-exist: there is an interplay between them. This is most impressively in evidence in the climactic passage in which Achilles chases Hector around the walls of Troy, then finally kills him. The

chase (XXII 131–213) is remarkable in its own right: it has probably
the least stylisation and the most immediacy of any passage in the
Iliad. Hector stands alone outside the walls; Achilles approaches;
Hector is terrified and takes to flight (131–7). Like a falcon swoop-
ing on a dove, Achilles pursues him (138–43) – and suddenly, after
this forceful, but conventional and conventionally styled, simile, the
narrative takes on a unique specificity and detail:

> past the look-out post they sped and the windy fig-tree, along a
> waggon-track away from the wall; and they reached two fair-flowing
> springs, from which the two sources of eddying Scamander well up. One
> runs with warm water, and fumes come off it as if it were a fire blazing;
> the other even in summer runs like hail or cold snow or ice.
>
> (145–52)

Of these landmarks, some have been mentioned before, for instance
the fig-tree (VI 433, XI 167), but the description of a setting for
heroic action in such detail is unprecedented. More remarkable still
is what follows:

> And there, near those same springs, are washing-tanks, broad, fine,
> stone, where the wives and the fair daughters of the Trojans used to wash
> their bright clothes in the time of peace, before the sons of the Achaeans
> came. Past there they ran, one in flight, one in pursuit behind.
>
> (153–7)

The clothes may be typically bright and the daughters typically fair;
almost everything else is individual and its immediacy is overwhelm-
ing. No such flights and pursuits normally occur in Homer: even if
they did, this one would be very special, and its special significance
calls forth a very distinctive style and mode of realism. Not only is
there a particularised setting. The shift to the present tense, in the
context of this wholly untypical particularity, produces a dramatic
effect of shrinking distance (as nowhere else in Homer, we seem to
be *there*), which the switch back to the past ('*used to wash*') duly
reverses: poignant glimpse of peace, reinstated distance.

And now Homer gives us a unique simile: Hector and Achilles ran
'for the life of Hector' like horses in a race running for a prize, and
(in exquisitely simple Greek) 'all the gods were watching' (*theoì d'es*

pántes horônto) (158–66: see pp. 90f.). The pursuit continues with 'swift Achilles' (188, 193) still close to his man – and, with its special applicability to the context, the great hero's habitual designation as 'swift' acquires a startling presence. Meanwhile Homer offers us another simile, menacing but, this time, more conventional: a dog chases a fawn and *must* eventually catch it – and Hector, though still ahead, cannot escape (188–98). And now a wholly unconventional simile follows: 'As in a dream <someone> can't catch <someone> escaping, the one can't catch, the other can't escape' – so Achilles could not catch Hector, nor Hector escape Achilles (199–201). The vehicle of the simile is unique in subject; it is also strikingly plain, even colloquial, in phraseology, with its simple diction and its informal assumption of grammatical subject and object; it impresses us as unformulaic; and together with the tenor it is also intensely patterned in sound:

> *hōs d'en oneírōi ou dúnatai pheúgonta diôkein:*
> *oút' ár' ho tòn dúnatai hupopheúgein oút' ho diôkein:*
> *hôs ho tòn ou dúnato márpsai posín, oud' hòs alúxai.*

Ordinary words, echo after echo, like an incantation:

> *dúnatai/dúnatai/dúnato, pheúgonta/hupopheúgein, diôkein/diôkein,*
> *ou/oút' . . . ho tón/oút' ho/ho tòn ou/oud' hós.*

In dreamlike repetitions the dream image is acted out hypnotically – but the dream, like all dreams, comes to an end. Apollo had kept Hector going. They reach the springs for the fourth time and (in accordance with Fate, as symbolised by the scales of Zeus) Apollo leaves Hector, and his death is at hand (208–13).

Viewed as a whole, the passage, 131–213, abounds in stylised features, but contains several sequences which by Homeric standards are strikingly free from them and, partly for that reason, confer an extraordinary presence and specificity on the scene. The section that now follows, culminating in the duel and Hector's death (214–366), is full of action and intensity, but by comparison with the astonishing passage before it, represents a shift back towards the stylised, the typical, the predictable. Hector's death is indeed predictable and we are able, therefore, to perceive the contrast between the stylised (more predictable) and the immediate (less predictable) as a dynamic one: there is, in other words, a correlation between the poem's organisation on the levels of structure and style.

The washing-tanks, mentioned only for the chase around Troy, and the generic epithet 'white' in 'white bones' might seem to be polar opposites. In fact they share one important quality, which helps to explain how it is that the *Iliad* can be so immediate and so stylised at the same time. The specified whiteness of Erymas' bones (XVI 347) does not differentiate them from his other bones or from other people's bones. For this reason, such epithets are sometimes called 'decorative'; however, the label totally distorts their significance. Bones have many possible qualities: the generic epithet 'white' points to one *representative* quality of all bones. The washing-tanks, similarly, are representative of various physical objects past which Hector, and then Achilles, might have run – objects belonging to ordinary life, rather than to the war – objects, therefore, evocative of the whole world of peacetime that has been undermined by this war and (from a Trojan point of view) especially by this chase.

'White', then, represents the qualities of bones; the washing-tanks represent the world of peace. This is more than a play on the word 'represent'. In both cases we are dealing with a symbolic technique, whereby significance, value and feeling are vested in exemplary concrete instances.

But why should the bones be generically white, and the instance of peace so specific? Because the generic and the specific alternate according to a clear principle: specificity is reserved for that which is *distinctively* significant. The poem offers us a 'predictable' background, against which, sharply defined, the special and the unique stand out in the foreground. For instance: the physical looks of the heroes are rarely described, unless referred to in their generic epithets (as Paris is habitually *theoeidés*, 'handsome as a god'); descriptions of them occur on special occasions, which their unusual specificity makes more special. So Agamemnon's looks are described in a series of similes (three short and one long) at the end of the unique cluster that leads up to the great catalogue of forces (II 477ff.). Agamemnon again, and other top Achaean heroes with him, are described by Priam in the unique scene with Helen on the walls of Troy

before the first duel (III 166ff.). An ordinary man's looks are described only if he improperly thrusts himself into the heroic lime-
light, as the mischief-maker Thersites does:

> The most obnoxious rogue who went to Troy,
> Bow-legged, with one limping leg, and shoulders
> Rounded above his chest, he had a skull
> Quite conical, and mangy fuzz like mould.   (II 216ff., tr. Fitzgerald)

Hector's looks are nowhere mentioned until Achilles destroys them,
when he binds Hector's dead body to his chariot and drags it through
the dust, so that

> the dark tresses
> Flowed behind, and the head, so princely once,
> Lay back in dust.   (XXII 401ff., tr. Fitzgerald)

Typical experience is glorified, we note (p. 49); particular instances
are treated with less impartiality through a kind of expressionist
symbolism: Hector looks like the hero he was, Thersites like the
villain he shows himself to be.

Value and feeling are embodied in concrete instances; and at
certain heightened moments very special values and feelings are
involved. The Achaean ambassadors 'came to the huts and the ships
of the Myrmidons and found Achilles delighting his heart with his
shrill lyre, fair and richly wrought, with a silver bridge on it, which
he had taken from the spoils when he sacked the city of Eëtion. In this
lyre he was taking delight, and his song was *kléa andrôn*, the glorious
deeds of men, and Patroclus sat alone opposite in silence, waiting for
him to finish singing' (IX 185ff.). The description is distinctive and
its climax is the pithy phrase that sums up not only Achilles' 'song',
but the significance of his situation and, implicitly, *his* feeling about
it: *he*, the most glorious of all warriors, is away from the war where
kléa andrôn are achieved, and *he*, uniquely of all the heroes in the
poem, celebrates them, rather than achieves them. In a comparable
moment and a comparable description, Helen's consciousness of
the war she has brought on Troy is characterised: 'But Iris went as
a messenger to white-armed Helen . . . She found her in the hall,
weaving a great double tapestry in purple and putting in the many
contests between the horse-taming Trojans and the bronze-mailed

Achaeans, which they were enduring at the hands of Ares for her sake' (III 121ff.). In the same way, the doomed Hector's situation and feelings are alluded to through the washing-tanks: that is part of the poignancy of the passage, but a poignancy that, as in all these passages, depends on the inexplicitness of the allusion.

16 Heroism

Hector, Achilles and the other heroes, Trojan and Achaean, are conceived of as heroes first and Trojans or Achaeans next. The Achaeans are superior in might, and in this sense the poem is, as later Greeks were to take it, an expression of triumphant Hellenism (p. 3); but more fundamentally it is an expression of a heroic ideology which is served, impartially, by Achaeans and Trojans alike.

The basis of this ideology is a logical chain which links death, glory, art and immortality. Death is inescapable and final; therefore life is of irreplaceable value; yet certain acts, especially those that risk or incur death, can achieve the glory that outlives finite life, so long as they are perpetuated in art; it may even be that the gods themselves, whose distinctive characteristic is their freedom from mortality, encourage this process; at all events, we thus reclaim a kind of immortality from the clutches of mortality itself. This ideology was not invented for the *Iliad*. In part it must have been worked out centuries, even millennia, before, as is clear from parallels in other Indo-European literary traditions, like the Germanic, and from the evident antiquity of the actual Homeric phrase for 'immortal glory' (*kléos áphthiton*: Vedic Sanskrit *śrávaḥ ákṣitam*). Nevertheless, the *Iliad* articulates it in a particular way and to particular effect.

The various links in the chain are frequently made explicit: when Sarpedon tells Glaucus of death and glory (XII 322–8); when Achilles 'sings' the *kléa andrõn* (IX 189); when Helen, perpetuator of the war in her tapestry (III 125ff.), suggests that Zeus himself has engineered her affair with Paris, 'so that in time to come we may be a poet's theme [*aoídimoi*] for men of the future' (VI 357–8); above all, in two speeches by Achilles. The first of these is to Odysseus during the embassy scene. A man can have many things, Achilles tells Odysseus. A man can have trophies and spoils. What he cannot have is his life (*psukhḗ*), once it has left his body: 'my mother, the goddess

Thetis . . . tells me I have two destinies . . . If I stay here, waging war on Troy, my hope of home [*nóstos*] is lost, but I win immortal glory [*kléos áphthiton*]. If I get back home to my own land, fine glory [*kléos esthlón*] is lost, but my life will be long' (IX 401ff.). The second speech, which looks back to the first, comes when Achilles laments the death of Patroclus to his goddess mother and swears vengeance on Hector. That, says Thetis, is a fateful decision, for Achilles' own death is destined to follow straight after Hector's. Achilles' response is unambiguous: 'then let me die at once . . . For not even mighty Heracles escaped death . . . so too shall I . . . be laid in death: now let me win fine glory [*kléos esthlón*]' (XVIII 98–121). Achilles' decision to opt for perpetual glory instead of a modest perpetuation of life duly gives the *Iliad* its own 'poet's theme'. It serves also to sum up the relationship between this glory and the 'honour', the *timḗ*, that the heroes are so concerned to preserve (p. 25). *Timḗ* is primarily the esteem due to a man from his contemporaries in respect of his status; *kléos*, 'glory', is what he wins beyond his lifetime in return for special achievement. Achilles withdraws from the fighting because of an affront to his *timḗ*; he returns to win *kléos*.

With his unique choice of destinies Achilles is exceptional, but, quite apart from Achilles, there is clearly something exceptional about the heroes as such. They are not men like us. They are a paradigm for us and distinct from us. They have the opportunity, the ability and the courage to win *kléos* at the risk of death, as we do not: we look up (and back) to them, as Achilles looks to Heracles. The glorious heroes are mortal, like us, but not merely that. They are inhuman like lions or wolves, as so many similes assure us, or elemental like wild air or water or fire (e.g. XI 747, V 87, XIII 53) or, after all, like gods (e.g. V 438). They are mortal and so not actually gods, but whether in-human, sub-human (as the animal similes sometimes suggest), or seemingly super-human, they are remote from ordinary humanity. Whatever else they are, they are mightier than us, and except for occasional incidents like the Achaean trick in X, epic fighting is all might, in which the mightier army and the mightier warrior must and do prevail.

All in all, they belong with the gods, who duly favour them with a kind of direct contact not known in our world. But the distinction between heroes and gods still remains absolute, witness the cautionary tale of Diomedes in V. Inspired by Athene (1ff.), he causes havoc among the Trojans, then attacks and wounds the goddess Aphrodite when she intervenes on behalf of her son, Aeneas (311–51), and later, with Athene's physical assistance, does the same to the war-god Ares himself (825ff.). In the meantime, however, he maintains an assault on Aeneas with his own resources, although he knows that Aeneas has now come under Apollo's protection (433): 'three times then he leapt on Aeneas, straining to kill him, and three times Apollo thrust back his bright shield. But when he rushed on him a fourth time, like a god [*daímoni îsos*], Apollo, who acts at will, shouted threateningly: "Think, son of Tydeus, and give way! Strive not to have a god's ambition: the race of immortal gods and the race of men that walk on earth will never be the same"' (436ff.). 'Think and give way' is *phrázeo . . . kaì kházeo*: men must remember their place and stay in it, and the rhyme enforces the logic. Even one who is godlike, but not a god, knows it. However, he remains godlike, and acts as if he knows that too.

The heroes have scope to act and achieve as individuals. They are kings and princes, and the freedom of action they doubtless enjoy in their principalities is reproduced on the field of battle. The hero can be constrained by a god (as Diomedes is by Apollo), but not by any considerations of space, time, season, weather or superior numbers: he 'storms over the plain like a torrent', sweeping away whole battalions (Diomedes, V 87ff.). His wounds, if any, will quickly heal, and he is not subject to illness: it is only the common soldiers who catch the plague (I 51ff.). 'All that impinges on [his] sovereignty is, as it were, erased and extinguished' (Fränkel, 1975). Above all, he is not restricted by the disciplines of teamwork. The Trojans may be fighting for a communal cause and the Achaeans may be fighting to avenge a national disgrace, but for the most part the heroes on both sides fight as individuals, in pursuit of individual glory. Hence the prominence given to the decisive moment of an individual's death: it is the moment when the final allocation of glory is made.

Heroic ideology presupposes human mortality, and the importance of this ideology to the poem helps to explain Homer's suppression of those traditional beliefs that offered some promise of immortal life: chthonic religion and, in particular, the hero-cult (p. 27). It is significant that outside epic poetry, the word *hérōs*, which is Homer's word for 'hero', means an immortal man, a dead man supposed to be superhuman and worshipped as such. *Hḗrōs* in the *Iliad* means a living man, a great warrior in search of timeless *kléos*: the connection with immortality is implicit, but revealingly different.

17 War

If the *Iliad* was all heroism, it would embody one single attitude to war: war would mean fighting for glory. But heroism is not the whole, and other attitudes are present.

The most obvious is the sense of war as a source of suffering. This, in the first instance, is the view of the ordinary soldiers on both sides, who (with few exceptions, like Dolon in X and Thersites in II) remain anonymous. These are the ordinary men like us, who do not and cannot win *kléos áphthiton*, the Trojans and Achaeans who stood aside from Menelaus' duel with Paris 'and were glad, because they hoped they had finished with wretched war' (III 111–12), then, sensing a new turn of events, said to one another, 'evil war and the dread din of battle: here they come again' (IV 81ff.). The formular epithets here are revealing. War is 'wretched' (*oïzurós*) and 'evil' (*kakós*) and the battle-din 'dread' (*ainḗ*), and these and other pejorative epithets recur throughout the poem in the narrative and in speeches by characters of all kinds, heroes included. War (*pólemos*) is also 'painful' (*argáleos*), 'full of tears' (*polúdakrus*), 'man-slaying' (*phthisḗnora*); battle (*mákhē*) is 'bitter' (*drimeîa*), 'tearful' (*dakruóessa*), 'grievous'(*algeinḗ*); Ares, the war-god, is 'plague to man' (*brotoloigós*) and 'hateful' (*stugerós*). There is some formular phraseology on the heroic side, like 'into glorious battle' (*mákhēn es kudiáneiran*) – but the vocabulary of suffering predominates overwhelmingly.

More surprisingly, this vocabulary is sometimes developed by the heroes themselves. In XIII Menelaus kills the Trojan Pisander, and, as heroes are wont to do, exults over the corpse, but it is a strange exultation that turns into a tirade against the other side: you took my wife, now you want to set fire to our ships and kill us all – 'Father Zeus . . . all this is your doing by showing favour to these Trojan criminals [*hubristē̂isi*]. Their prowess is evil: they cannot get enough of the din of war. A man can have too much of anything – sleep, love, singing and dancing – and any man would rather have too much of these than of war, but the Trojans cannot get enough fighting' (631ff.). In IX Achilles himself, the supreme fighter, articulates a version of this attitude: no, Agamemnon will not persuade me to fight: what thanks did I ever get for fighting? –

> The man who waits and the man who fights have the same fate. The coward and the brave man share the same honour. They both die, the man who does nothing and the one who does it all. Suffering, forever staking my life in war, has got me nothing. As a bird brings her chicks all the bits and pieces she can find, though the going is hard for her, so I used to pass sleepless nights and battle my way through the bloody days, fighting men for their women.   (318ff.)

The strained analogy, along with the oblique reference to Helen and his own Briseis (once 'captured by his spear', IX 343, now taken from him by Agamemnon), reminds us that anger and hurt pride are determining this critique of heroic war. Even so, the critique is telling.

If even the heroes can see war as suffering, it is their families, above all, and themselves as members of those families, who experience the effects of war in these terms. In VI Hector meets Andromache inside Troy. She asks him to stay inside the city for his, and her, safety; 'Hector, you are my father, my lady mother, my brother, and my strong husband. Please have pity and stay here at the wall, or you will make your child an orphan and your wife a widow' (429ff.). Hector appeals to the heroic creed: what can he do? He would be ashamed to hide like a coward. Upbringing and inclination tell him always to fight out front, along with the top men of Troy, 'winning great glory' (446), his father's and his own. Then, with the directness and total absence of rhetoric that mark many speeches in the poem, he delineates her life ahead:

> The day will come when sacred Ilios is destroyed and Priam and the people of Priam . . . But it is not so much the pain of the Trojans in times to come that concerns me, nor even Hecabe's, nor King Priam's, nor the pain of my brothers, so many and so brave, who will be laid low in the dust by our enemies, but yours, when one of the bronze-mailed Achaeans leads you away in tears and takes away your day of freedom. And in Argos, it may be, you will weave at some other woman's loom

or carry water from Messeïs or Hypereia against your will, for strong necessity will be laid upon you. And some man will watch you weep and say: 'This is the wife of Hector, who was the best of the horsetaming Trojans when they fought around Troy.' So someone will say, and for you there will be new pain in your lack of a man like me to fend off the day of bondage.   (448ff.)

Andromache is holding the baby Astyanax. As he finishes speaking, Hector reaches to his son, but the child is frightened by the sight of his father in his exotic helmet. He cries; his parents laugh; and taking off the symbol of war, Hector gives the baby a kiss, holds him and prays that his son may become, like him, a mighty ruler of Ilios, so that

one day, when he comes home from war, someone may say of him, 'This one is far braver than his father.' May he kill his enemy and carry off the bloody spoils, and may his mother's heart be glad.   (479ff.)

In this justly famous passage two seemingly incompatible attitudes are presented in dynamic contrast, such that both are given their due and made to coexist. In particular, we note that the 'mother's heart' is to share in the sense of glory, just as the warrior Hector shares in his wife's impending sorrow: the attitudes are larger than the individuals who represent them, but still balanced.

The contrast between glory and suffering that informs the Hector–Andromache scene pervades the poem. It comes into sharp focus in the narrator's 'necrologies' that accompany many of the killings. In these concise and unsentimental statements, recitation of the victim's background, usually his family background, adds the necessary perspective to the winning and losing of glory in battle: 'With these words he shot another arrow from the string straight at Hector, eager to hit him. Hector he missed; Gorgythion he hit in the chest with his arrow, Priam's brave son by a woman from Aesyme, fair Castianeira, lovely as one of the goddesses' (VIII 300ff.). Above all, in this war poem whose narrative never shrinks from the war, we have what Simone Weil called 'brief evocations of the world of peace': vivid reminders of what life is, or was, without war. Sometimes the 'evocation' depends on an object of passing interest, like the washing-tanks in XXII. Once it depends on a special circumstance and a specially conceived object, Achilles' shield (p. 68). Most often it derives from similes that offer a poignant sense of the ordinary rhythm and felicity of a world without war in overt comparison to the world of war itself:

> All morning, while the holy day grew, the spears of each side found the other, and the men fell. But at the hour a woodman takes his meal in a mountain glade, when his arms are tired cutting down the tall trees and fatigue comes over him and he yearns for food, at that hour, by their valour, the Danaans broke through, calling to their comrades down the line.   (XI 84ff.)

In some cases the contrast implicit in the simile is extreme. Gorgythion's 'necrology' is completed by a simile of this kind: 'Priam's brave son . . . dropped his head to one side like a poppy in a garden, laden with fruit and the spring rain: just so his head bowed, weighed down by his helmet' (VIII 303ff.). Fruit and spring, life and growth: the irony is profound.

In modern discussions of Homer, such contrastive similes are sometimes trivialised as moments of 'relief' or 'variety' from the endless fighting. Rather, the endlessness of the fighting and the contrastive evocations of the similes are equal and necessary truths, mutually explicating each other; and within this relationship the similes work on a vastly deeper level than 'relief' or 'variety' suggests.

War means glory, war means suffering. And in the *Iliad* war also means something very unfashionable in our generation, a magnificent event, the thought and sight of which has a tonic effect. A representative moment is the description of Paris emerging from Troy to rejoin battle, a passage which has the greater force in that it directly follows the Hector – Andromache scene:

> Nor did Paris linger in his high house, but buckled on his splendid armour . . . and ran through the city, sure-footed and swift. Like a well-fed stallion, shut in the manger, who breaks his halter and runs stamping for joy over the plain to the river with its fair streams where he likes to bathe – and he holds his head high and tosses his mane over his shoulders, and sure of his looks he makes quickly for the place where the horses pasture – so Paris, Priam's son, strode briskly down from the heights of Troy, with his armour bright like the blazing sun, laughing.
>   (VI 503ff.)

The physical challenge of the fight is shown to be the source of an intense vitality, which Paris already has in anticipation: his absorption in it is total. The pleasure we are invited to feel is more detached, but free from any irony. The detachment is a god's: 'and Athene and Apollo . . . sat in the likeness of eagles on the high oak of father Zeus . . . relishing the sight of the men' (VII 58ff.).

It has been argued (notably by Redfield) that war, though socially respectable, is also represented as anti-social, therefore is shown to be problematic. As a view of the *Iliad*, this is false. It is the product of a modern prejudice, natural enough in the light of our special experience of war in its horrific modern guises. War in the *Iliad* is a complex entity, but it is accepted by the narrator and his characters, and offered to us, as a norm. The participants feel no bitterness on its account. Hector tells Paris off, but more for inertia than for bringing war to Troy (III 39ff., VI 520ff.). Priam (XXII 41ff.) – and Hecabe too (XXIV 212–13) – may detest Achilles for his cruelty, but Priam's supplication seems still to imply Achilles' entitlement to kill 'so many of his sons' (XXIV 477–521). Even Achilles in IX is not bitter about war itself, but rather about heroism (p. 65). The gods too accept war, 'relishing the sight of the men' (VII 61).

These various attitudes to war are encapsulated in Achilles' shield, handiwork of the god Hephaestus (XVIII 468ff.). On it are five segments (481), evidently circles, each with a different scene. At the centre are the earth, the sky and the sea (483ff.). Outside the central circle are two cities, one at peace, busy with a marriage and a law-suit, the other at war, suffering siege, and preparing an ambush against its attackers, while the old men, the women and the children are left inside the city wall (490ff.). The third circle contains the seasons of the rural year (541ff.), the fourth a dance (590ff.), and the fifth, 'around the outermost rim', Ocean (670ff.). The whole is a microcosm that begins with the elements and is enclosed by Ocean, which in Greek myth is a river that encloses the world. The natural elements, therefore, occupy the beginning and the end, and within them is human life, lived according to the seasons and social custom, and represented as a unified whole. Within that whole, alongside civil disputes and social celebrations, war has a proper place – war in two guises: the ambush and the siege, technique and might, the kind of war the *Iliad* ignores and the kind the *Iliad* is about.

In this unexpectedly long perspective, almost an allegorical commentary on the poem itself, we miss the glory and the exhilaration of war, but we see its threatening implications for the weak (the women, the old, the young); we see war placed against alternative experience; and we are also aware of this whole 'allegory' as itself a weapon of war, made into an artistic spectacle by a god for the use of the supreme warrior. Readers, or listeners, are left to draw their own conclusions.

18 Gods and men

At the start of I, the heroes quarrel on earth; at the end of I, the gods quarrel on Olympus. In essence, both quarrels are about *timē*, honour: Achilles feels himself dishonoured by Agamemnon, as Hera does by Zeus' promise to Thetis (514–21, 536–43). But the parallel at once becomes a contrast. The heroes' quarrel is set to bring death and destruction; the gods', by comparison, is aimless and even frivolous. On earth no reconciliation is possible until most of the damage has been done. In heaven the lame god Hephaestus is able to divert Hera's rage with a cautionary tale against himself (586ff.) and a display of his disability: 'and unquenchable laughter arose among the blessed gods at the sight of Hephaestus bustling through the palace' (599–600). Our first sight of a god in the *Iliad* was less amusing. Apollo comes for his vengeance on the Achaeans, and – 'down from the peaks of Olympus he strode in his anger, with his bow and quiver on his shoulders, and on his shoulders the arrows rattled as the angry god pressed on, and his coming was like the night' (I 44ff.). The Hephaestus scene serves to show us that however serious the gods may be on earth, in heaven they represent what Karl Reinhardt has called 'sublime triviality'. It is the siting of the ludicrous theomachy *on earth* that makes the episode jar (*cf.* p. 39). The spectacle of (for instance) Ares flattened by a cackling Athene (XXI 406ff.) might be tolerable as *grand guignol* in heaven: on earth it seems quite improper.

Even without such special moments, however, the gods turn out to have less than a heroic dignity. They are more powerful than men, more beautiful (with exceptions, like Hephaestus) and, being immortal, free from the disfigurements of age and decay; but on any human value-scale they are less than the heroes, who have the capacity and the will to risk their lives in the quest for glory: as unchanging immortals, the gods have less to lose and therefore less to win. This superiority of heroes to gods rightly struck one thoughtful critic in later antiquity as paradoxical: 'Homer has done his best to make the men in the *Iliad* gods and the gods men' ('Longinus', *On the Sublime*, ix 7).

The gods present a parallel sphere and a pantheon of parallel characters: what they do not present is a fully independent action. They may play a part in determining the course of human affairs, but within the poem they have few affairs of their own to determine. Their acts are essentially responses to developments on the earthly stage, like Zeus' response to Achilles' humiliation in I. To this extent, the gods of the *Iliad* belong not to any theology, but to a religious anthropology.

The poem's primary field of action, therefore, is human; and the gods – in another of their main activities – observe it. Our life is their spectacle, especially when life offers a spectacle as magnificent as the Trojan war. Zeus, above all, is the great spectator: 'I shall stay here, sitting on a ridge of Olympus, where I can watch and enjoy. But you other gods go down among the Trojans and Achaeans, and help whichever side you have a mind to' (XX 22ff.). Human sufferings are accepted without question as part of the natural order, and Zeus can enjoy them. At the same time, his enjoyment may be complicated by foreknowledge of the outcome and by feelings of pity for the participants: 'But when Zeus saw [Hector] putting on the armour [of Achilles] . . . he shook his head and said to himself: "Poor man, death is not in your thoughts, but how close it is coming to you!"' (XVII 198ff.). The foreknowledge and the pity clearly belong together: it is because Zeus knows the outcome that he feels pity. For a hero to be pitied by a divine spectator is a compliment, for only the great are so favoured, but the compliment is not an assurance of survival: Sarpedon, like Hector, is pitied by Zeus (XVI 431ff.), but by the end of the poem both are destroyed.

These divine spectators, however, are also higher powers which exert themselves for or against us: their aesthetic pleasure is matched by their innumerable interventions in the action. Here Zeus clearly has the main say, which begins with his decision to honour Achilles by assisting the Trojans (I 495–528, II 1ff.) and ends with his insistence that Achilles return Hector's body to Priam (XXIV 64ff., 103ff.). And it is in the course of his encounter with Priam that it falls to Achilles to articulate, in pessimistic terms, the cumulative effectiveness of Zeus' power over us:

> Chill lament brings no gain. This is how the gods ordained man's destiny, to live in pain, while they have no afflictions. At Zeus' door are set two urns, of good and of evil gifts. To some, Zeus gives both kinds: then they have misfortune sometimes, good fortune sometimes. To some, he gives only the evil: then they are ruined . . . dishonoured . . .   (XXIV 524ff.)

The *Iliad* also makes it clear that over a wide area of behaviour and experience, the gods are to be thought of as sources of permanent human faculties and – especially – momentary human impulses. The poet prays to the Muse, because in order to compose he needs not only his fundamental 'gift' (as we still call it) but the god-given inspiration of the moment; and this is the pattern for many special decisions and experiences. An angry Achilles thinks of killing Agamemnon, but decides against it, and the decision is prompted by Athene (I 193ff.). Diomedes charges into the thick of the fighting to win glory, prompted again by Athene (V 1ff.). Glaucus perversely gives Diomedes gold armour in exchange for bronze, because Zeus has 'taken away his wits' (VI 234ff.). Hector, pursued by swift Achilles, manages, against all the odds, to keep ahead – 'and how could Hector have escaped the fates of death, if Apollo, for the very last time, had not come close to rouse his strength?' (XXII 202ff.) – but then Zeus lifts his scales, Hector's fate sinks, 'and Phoebus Apollo left him' (XXII 213), from which moment his effort cannot be sustained.

Such instances of divine interference are not strictly miraculous. There are indeed some interventions which could only be described in these terms. When Aphrodite snatches Paris away from the bat-tlefield (III 380ff.) to the bafflement of Menelaus (449ff.), or when Apollo preserves Hector's mangled body from disfigurement (XXIV 18ff.), we have a supernatural agency defying natural laws. But Achilles' decision to let Agamemnon live, Diomedes' great charge, Glaucus' momentary lapse and Hector's final spurt are moments that are recognisably human, moments of unusual human effort or behaviour. In such cases the gods may still be sources of the special impulse, but they are also symbols of it. Though consistently and

coherently represented as external beings, they constitute forces
which, in such cases, we may take as equally internal. The human
sphere, in effect, is re-interpreted, not disrupted; and the distinction
is important. The *Iliad* celebrates individual human achievement,
which would be devalued if the achievement 'really' was a god's and
not *also* the hero's own. The consequent 'double determination' duly
finds its way into Homeric vocabulary: a man will achieve 'when
his heart bids him and a god rouses him' (IX 702–3). So achievement is not diminished by its divine associations; rather, they serve
to symbolise its special authority and distinction. The *Iliad* offers a
projection of heroic autonomy, but on divine ground.

All in all, the gods are central to the poem, because it is they who
set the heroes' engagements in relief and invest them with meaning. In the first place, they evoke a higher magnificence to which
the 'godlike' heroes, in their confrontations with death, aspire. Then
again, the gods' interest in heroic endeavour guarantees its splendour, as well as its poignancy. Above all, these same splendid gods
serve to show why human death is necessary. They are splendid,
but also trivial, and we die lest we be trivial like them. This is the
crucial implication of the squabbles in I. The human argument leads
to suffering and death; the divine argument has no consequences.
The human is seen to matter in a way that the divine cannot.

19 The characters and their presentation

Like so much else in the *Iliad*, its human figures are strikingly immediate and alive – and yet strikingly different from their modern
equivalents. Our literary notions of immediacy and life are derived
from the characters of modern fiction. Homer's Achilles, we shall see,
is a special case, but his characters, even Achilles, are not like ours.

As a group, Homer's characters are less representative of the
world at large than ours are likely to be. They are largely adult males
of unspecified age but in their prime, drawn from a restricted social
class and existing in a restricted environment. The aged counsellor
Nestor and the old king Priam, the baby Astyanax and the women,
Helen, Hecabe and Andromache – all these play their parts, but the
main figures are heroes at war, preoccupied with their own and each
other's prowess: 'And Agamemnon caught him by the hand and said:
"You are mad, Menelaus . . . You cannot think of fighting Hector . . .

Even Achilles shrinks from facing him in battle, and he is much better than you"' (VII 107ff.). Minor warriors come and go. More ordinary mortals are few and far between: the herald Talthybius, the priest Chryses, the girl Briseis, the upstart Thersites; most are not even mentioned by name.

In any case, Homer's people are not presented exactly as we might have presented them. In the first place, like characters in early Greek literature in general, they appear less as private, inward individuals than as accessible beings whose identity is defined primarily by their public or external status. Agamemnon is an individual with an individual's feelings, but first and foremost he is a 'king of men' who *behaves* as a king. Minor figures tend to be nothing but their status. Agamemnon's herald, Talthybius, is what a herald is and does what a herald does: no more and no less. Even a figure of Hecabe's importance is largely summed up by her roles as Priam's wife and Hector's mother. When we hear her voicing her anxiety for Hector alive (VI 254ff.) or her grief for Hector dead (XXII 431ff.), or her concern, again, for Priam (XXIV 201ff.), her feelings are convincing, but they are feelings limited to, and co-ordinate with, this status. It is symptomatic that the *Iliad* should contain no romance. This is not because the conception of romance is unknown to the author and his milieu – even romance between 'girl and boy, girl and boy' (XXII 127–8). Nor is there any shortage of possible couples. Hera seduces Zeus; Achilles (some of the time) sleeps with Briseis; Paris and Helen share an intense physical attraction, as we see in III; Hector and Andromache are a more balanced man and wife; Achilles and Patroclus are close friends and comrades-at-arms. But there are no romantic 'relationships' here, no 'true love', and above all none of the hard personal decisions that we associate with such commitments. We value the inward, therefore we tend to place a special value on crises of conscience, wherever they occur, and therefore we expect to explore an individual's hesitations and uncertainties: in this respect Hamlet (as Hegel saw, around two centuries ago) is the ideal representative of modern literature. Hesitancy is not unheard-of in the *Iliad* – witness Phoenix in IX (p. 35) – but the usual pattern with Homer's characters is a quite un-modern decisiveness. Take, for instance, Patroclus, faced with Nestor's plea to save the Achaeans in Achilles' stead (XI 655–68, 790–803). A modern Patroclus might be racked by conflicting loyalties: Homer's

Patroclus has his response ready on the spot (XI 804), and reports it to Achilles with no sign of mixed feelings (XVI 2–45). His inward inclinations are as clear-cut as his princely exterior, and the two are so closely attuned as to sound as one.

Yet this does not mean that the characters have no unseen inner life. In XXIV Priam prepares a carriage-load of gifts for Achilles in readiness for his dangerous mission to reclaim Hector's body. He shouts to his sons to help. They have the misfortune not to be Hector; every one of them is a disgrace; and he upbraids them in almost the homespun tones of the pioneer: 'cheats and dancers, just dandy at foot-tapping, busy snatching lambs and kids from your own folk' (261–2). His bluster (and the Greek has a marvellous sequence of unexpected dismissive assonance, *pseûstaí t' orkhēstaí te khoroitupíēisin áristoi*) conceals, but implies, his emotions. The emotion is left to be inferred from the words – just as, with more complex feelings, Hector's are from the washing-tanks, Achilles' from his lyre, Helen's from her tapestry (pp. 57, 60f.). Psychological complexities (as we would think of them) may or may not be involved; in either case, the inward corresponds to the outward and is implicit in it.

Granted *both* the restricted environment within which Homer's people operate *and* an emphasis on the public and the external, it is inevitable that there are no rounded characters in the poem. Individuals are presented and differentiated in very partial terms, in some cases simply through their martial capabilities: we think of Teucer as the hero with the bow, we distinguish Diomedes and Ajax as offensive and defensive fighters. The characters are not 'men like us' with a multiplicity of traits and interests, let alone idiosyncrasies or contradictions: when Glaucus behaves gratuitously, by giving Diomedes gold for bronze (VI 234ff.), it is made clear that this is a momentary aberration ('Zeus took away his wits'). They are homogeneous and consistent representatives of one or two particular qualities: Patroclus, generous and noble; Nestor, wise but long-winded; Agamemnon, physically courageous, morally weak. Odysseus (as more than one of his stock epithets reminds us) is shrewd and politically adroit: the man who brings the assembly to order in II (244ff.); the man chosen to make the first approach to Achilles in IX (179ff., 222ff.); the man who curbs Achilles' impetuous eagerness to fight in XIX (154ff.) by pointing out the army's need for food. Achilles himself is an altogether exceptional figure in the *Iliad*, yet he too has his main trait: he is swift – physically and psychologically – and the motivation of the whole poem depends on it: a different temperament would have reacted more cautiously to Agamemnon's insistence on compensation for Chryseis (I 101ff., 121ff.) and even to his threat to secure it by dispossessing Achilles himself (I 130ff., 148ff.).

The individualisation of the characters is in any case subordinated to their representative status in another, higher, sense. The *Iliad* alternates between descriptions in which we stay at an even distance from the events and the people described, and what are in effect close-ups on particular people in special situations. These moments tend to involve pairs of people and to touch on issues of life and death. They are supreme representative encounters, and the people involved in them acquire a supreme representative quality in their turn. In VI Hector and Andromache talk not of themselves or each other as unique individuals, but of the universal conditions of glory and widowhood: their meeting is a classic articulation of human feeling, not a revelation of human variety. The same is true of Hector and Achilles with their shared enmity (XXII) and Achilles and Priam with a more surprising shared humanity (XXIV). There are, it is true, other pairings articulated in a different way, with a series of meetings or shared situations instead of a single decisive encounter. In Achilles and Patroclus, Achilles and Agamemnon, Helen and Paris, Paris and Hector, we sense relationships which might, if we were ever told, embody a wide area of individual feeling and response. But we never are told; and the glimpses of, for instance, Hector and his brother remain as partial as they are vivid. 'Depravity-Paris, good-looking, sex-mad seducer' is how Hector's first speech to his brother begins (III 39), but we are never to know much more about the 'reality' that might lie behind, or might qualify, this rhetoric.

Perhaps the most alien feature of Homer's people is that, in general, they seem to show no capacity for development: character is conceived as static. Individuals, no doubt, are presumed to grow up and grow old and, in the process, to acquire the habits appropriate to each stage of life, but within the poem they are fully-formed when they appear and seem unaffected by any subsequent experience. The Achaeans are driven almost to despair by Hector's onslaught (XI–XVI), but once the tide has turned, none of them shows any psychological scars. Agamemnon offers Achilles a public apology for the dishonour he did him, but he gives no sign of having learned any lesson: 'I am not to blame, but Zeus and Fate and the avenging Fury that walks in the mist . . . they cast wild madness [*átē*] on my soul . . . But what could I do? A god can make anything happen' (XIX 86ff.). For the record, this is not how the narrative represented Agamemnon's act of will in I, and the discrepancy might be construed as a negative comment on Agamemnon himself. But the very fact that acts of human will *can* be ascribed to divine intervention tends to deprive their agents of the sense of full autonomy on which development, as we understand it, depends. Even the conscious experience of such divine interventions seems to leave no permanent effect. Diomedes encounters Apollo in his path: '"Think and give way . . .",', Apollo tells him (V 440), and he duly gives way, 'avoiding the wrath' of the god (443–4); but shortly afterwards he is fighting as normal again. Athene comes to assist him, and he recognises her – 'I know you, daughter of Zeus' (V 815) – but once again the experience of the encounter leaves nothing discernible behind. God keeping man to his limits, god inspiring man to action, are represented as objective embodied truths, not as a matter of personal experience, in our terms, at all.

20 Achilles

Unseen, great Priam came in, and standing close to Achilles took hold of his knees and kissed his hands, the grim man-slaying hands that had killed so many of his sons. And . . . Achilles was astonished at the sight of godlike Priam, and the others were astonished too, and they looked at each other. But Priam appealed to him: 'Remember your father, godlike Achilles. His years are as mine: he stands on the deathly threshold of old age. He too, it may be, is hard pressed by those around him, with no one to defend him from ruin and destruction. But at least he can hear that you are still alive, and be glad, and hope every day to see his son return from Troy. But utter misfortune is all I have: I had sons who were the noblest men in broad Troy, and not one of them, I tell you, is

left . . . The one who stood alone, guarding the city and its people, you
killed the other day . . . It is for Hector that I am here now . . . I bring vast
ransom. Respect the gods, Achilles, and pity me. Remember your own
father. Well, I am more to be pitied: I have brought myself to do what no
one else has ever done: lifted to my lips the hand of the man who killed
my son.' These were his words, and Achilles was moved by them to weep
for his father. And he took the old man by the hand and gently pushed
him back. So the two of them remembered and wept: Priam wept for
man-slaying Hector, as he huddled at Achilles' feet; Achilles wept for his
own father and then for Patroclus; and their cries filled the room. But
when great Achilles had had his indulgence of tears . . . he left his seat
and taking the old man by the hand, made him get up, pitying his grey
head and his grey beard, and he said: 'Poor man, your heart has borne
so much pain . . . Come on, sit on a chair. Let our sorrows lie still in our
hearts, for all our grief. Chill lament brings no gain. This is how the gods
ordained man's destiny, to live in pain, while they have no afflictions. At
Zeus' door are set two urns, of good and of evil gifts . . . To some, Zeus
gives both . . . To some, only the evil . . . To Peleus [Achilles' father],
the gods gave glorious gifts . . . so that he surpassed all men in wealth
and happiness . . . Yet on him too a god has brought suffering: he had
no family . . . of royal sons, but instead one son utterly out of season
[*panaōrios*]. And he grows old, and I give him no support, squatting here
at Troy, far from home, afflicting you and your children. And you were
once blessed, old man, we know . . . with wealth and sons. But ever since
the gods in heaven brought this sorrow on you, you have fighting and
killing around your city . . .' The old man, godlike Priam, answered: 'No
chair for me, my lord, so long as Hector lies in your camp uncared for.
Give him back now, and let me see him. Take all these gifts we bring and
enjoy them. You have spared me. I pray you reach your own land.' But
swift Achilles glared and said: 'Provoke me no more, old man. I mean
to give you Hector anyway: a messenger from Zeus came to me . . . and
I know . . . that some god brought you . . . So now beware my temper.
I have my own sorrows. Get at me any more, and I may not spare you,
old man, but may sin against the commandment of Zeus, for all that you
are a suppliant under my own roof.' So he spoke, and the old man was
frightened and did as he was told. But like a lion the son of Peleus sprang
out of the room . . . And he called the maids and told them to wash the
body and anoint it, but some way off, in case Priam should see his son
and be distressed and not restrain his anger, and Achilles should lose his
temper himself and kill him against the commandment of Zeus.

(XXIV 477–586)

This magnificent passage, whose force survives translation and excerpting, is quoted at length to make one point in particular: Achilles is special. He weeps with wretched Priam, his enemy, as they share their different griefs. Priam begs: 'Give him back now . . . I pray you reach your own land.' Achilles' response is terrifying, and Priam is terrified: he reacts to the 'swift' man that Achilles is. But Achilles' response, though 'swift', is more than that. We know, as Priam does not, that there are depths behind Achilles' words, and what they are. We know that his angry response is not some 'natural' malevolence, but reflects a sensitivity associated with an exceptional moral position and an exceptional awareness. Achilles killed Hector to avenge Patroclus. Patroclus' death was his responsibility, for which only that revenge-killing could make amends. By that revenge, however, Achilles has ensured, in full consciousness, that he cannot, as Priam magnanimously hopes, reach his homeland again. This is his personal sorrow, which, out of consideration for Priam, he declines to articulate, however painful such silence must be for a 'plain-speaking' hero (p. 55); his anger reflects that pain and the underlying sorrow in one. All of which makes Achilles, and his presentation, unique in the *Iliad*.

Achilles is the only character in the poem to be explored in any depth. He is the only character who can really be shown to possess such depth. Why this should be is a matter for speculation, but we may note: that Achilles motivates the action of the poem, and is, therefore, a focus of interest in his own right; that his specific decision to withdraw from the fighting requires him to articulate his already unusual situation, and so reveal himself to himself, as others are never required to; that it is an exceptional and extreme self that he reveals; but that without the special pressures of war (we infer) even this exceptional person would not be brought to this revelation.

This exceptional hero has a suitably special, even alien, background. His mother is a sea-nymph and he was brought up by a centaur, Chiron (XI 831–2). And during the action these alien connections are evoked by his god-made weapons (XVIII), his talking horse (XIX 404ff.), his fight with a river (XXI 211ff.).

By background, he is alien; by temperament, swift. He becomes an outsider. The key-word for understanding him is the surprising word he applies to himself in the Priam scene: *panaōrios*: a word seemingly coined for this context, and hinting at an untimely death, but in itself meaning 'utterly out of season', therefore at odds with natural rhythms and norms.

Unlike his great enemy Hector, the outsider Achilles is rootless. He has no family near him and no friends, except for one close friend. We see him leave the war, then rejoin the war, as the individualist hero *par excellence*; and before he rejoins the war, we see him sitting on the sea-shore on his own (I 349–50), spurning the assembly where men meet, as well as the war where they fight (I 490–1); we even see him, with Patroclus as his silent audience, playing the convivial lyre on his own (IX 186ff.).

And the outsider becomes an extremist in all things. On hearing the news of Patroclus' death, he tears his hair and rolls in ashes (XVIII 22ff.), and days later he is still refusing food and sex with his woman, Briseis (XXIV 128ff.). And yet he is as intense a lover of Briseis as he was a friend of Patroclus, whom he honoured as he honoured himself (XVIII 81–2). When she is taken from him, he grieves for her (II 694); he calls her his wife, his darling (*álokhon thumaréa*, IX 336); she was only the spoils of war, but he loved her from the heart (*ek thumoû phíleon*, IX 343). When Hector acknowledges his supremacy and supplicates him, his response is to wish he could eat his enemy alive (XXII 346–7), and his actual treatment of Hector's body scandalises the gods (XXIV 107ff.). His refusal to accept Agamemnon's generous settlement violates expectation and precedent, as Phoenix (IX 496ff., 515ff.) and Ajax (IX 628ff.) make clear.

With his extreme temperament and his propensity for isolation, Achilles finds himself in a unique situation. The greatest of the heroes becomes the most obdurate anti-hero; but the heroic life provides no practice in opting out of wars, and by opting out of this war, Achilles exposes himself to contradictory feelings, which he expresses by contradictory actions. Withdrawn to his tent, he longs for the war (I 492), but he also longs for home: his speech to Odysseus in the embassy-scene contains a plaintive fantasia on the theme of a marriage in his native 'Hellas and Phthia' (IX 393ff.). Athene stays his hand against Agamemnon with the promise of great gifts in the future (I 213–14); when Agamemnon offers them, he scorns them

(IX 260ff., 378ff.); later, the same gifts seem to be uppermost in his thoughts (XVI 84ff.); finally, when he does decide to rejoin the war, and Agamemnon assures him that the promised gifts will still be his (XIX 140–1), they seem, after all, hardly to concern him (XIX 147–8). Before Patroclus' death he entertains the wish that the whole Achaean army should perish along with Troy, and that he and Patroclus alone should survive (XVI 97ff.); after Patroclus' death he laments that he gave no assistance to Patroclus himself *or* to his other comrades (XVIII 102–3). Briseis is his 'wife', his 'darling' (IX 336); but when he makes his peace with Agamemnon, she is just 'a girl' (*koúrē*) who should have died the day he first captured her, and saved so many Achaean lives (XIX 56ff.). Even his extreme actions may oscillate, contradictorily, from one extreme to another. Once he was humane to his defeated opponents (VI 414ff.) and even granted their supplications (XXI 100ff.); after Patroclus' death he kills all his victims (XXI 103ff.) and kills and mutilates the supplicant Hector (XXII 337ff., 395ff.); after Hector's death, humanity returns, and he responds to Priam's entreaties, which no other hero in fact does for a defeated enemy in the *Iliad*.

Our understanding of this extraordinary character is enhanced by an unusual amount of information about his background. His own speeches provide much of this, but we hear a good deal also from less predictable sources, like Andromache (VI 414ff.), Phoenix (IX 485ff.), Nestor (XI 762ff.), and Odysseus, who chooses to remind Achilles of Peleus' cautionary words on his son's combative spirit (IX 254ff.) which is so evident in the quarrel in I. Above all, we learn from Achilles himself about his fate, his awareness of that fate, and the unique personal crisis that this awareness represents, a crisis of choice and even – in this one instance – a crisis of conscience, to which all his contradictory feelings and actions can be traced: 'my mother . . . tells me I have two destinies . . . If I stay here, waging war on Troy, my hope of home is lost, but I win immortal glory. If I get back home to my own land, fine glory is lost, but my life will be long . . .' (IX 410ff.). Possessed of this knowledge, Achilles must choose. His original inclination must have been to choose glory and a short life at Troy. The strength of his grudge against Agamemnon leads him towards the alternative. In his speech to Odysseus in IX he actually talks as if he has now opted for life: 'tomorrow I shall . . . load my ships and put to sea, and at daybreak, if you care to look, you will see them sailing over the Hellespont' (357ff.). However, his next speech, to Phoenix, leaves it open: 'at daybreak we shall decide whether to go home or stay' (618–19). And his next, to Ajax, is different again. He is apparently thinking of staying put after all, but – 'I will not bother myself with bloody war until great Hector . . . kills his way to the huts and the ships of the Myrmidons, and sets the ships on fire' (650ff.). Whether this plan, which he later reaffirms to Patroclus (XVI 61ff.), was always his underlying intention, we are not invited to consider. What is significant is the sequence of contradictory positions, so eloquent of the great hero's indecision. The plan is, in any case, not to be realised: it is Patroclus who re-enters the war in Achilles' stead, when Hector does fire the first ship, and Achilles himself joins in only later to avenge his friend. That belated re-entry, however, marks his final decision to die at Troy, and is so interpreted both by Achilles' goddess mother (XVIII 95–6) and by Achilles himself: 'Let me die at once [98] . . . My fate I shall accept when Zeus and the other immortal gods will it to be fulfilled [115–16] . . . Now let me win fine glory' (121).

Released from his indecision, Achilles kills *his* way to fine glory, but the consciousness of his own fate to come weighs on him, even as he kills. Lycaon, one of his victims and another of Priam's sons, supplicates him (XXI 74ff.). Achilles' response is disconcertingly impartial:

> no man that a god puts into my hands at Troy shall escape death, not one man of Troy and least of all any son of Priam. No, my friend, you die too. Why sob like that? Patroclus died, and he was a better man than you, by far. And me: you see my looks, my greatness? My father was a noble man, my mother was a goddess – but death and the power of fate are on me too: a morning or an evening or a noon will come, when some man takes my life in battle with a cast of the spear or an arrow from the bow.   (XXI 103ff.)

Achilles' special consciousness is not confined to his own fate. When a hero is dying and making his death-speech, he is often credited with a kind of momentary insight such as a god might possess – as if the human spirit, on its way from earth to the divine, if dismal, realms of the underworld, experienced a flash of divine omniscience. So Hector, as he dies, warns Achilles of 'that day when Paris and Phoebus Apollo will kill you, for all your greatness, at the Scaean gate' (XXII 359–60). Achilles alone enjoys, or suffers, that special insight while he still lives, and in his confrontation with Priam in XXIV this insight at last takes a positive form. In the image of the urns of Zeus, it translates itself into a profound statement about the human condition, which no one else is fitted to articulate; and it is informed by a powerful humanity, which could hardly have been greater if Priam had been the father that Achilles knows he will never see again. For with his consciousness of life, Achilles gains a rare self-awareness, typified by the elaborate manoeuvre with the body which is designed to ensure that Priam does not unwittingly provoke him again (582ff.).

The special hero is special in another way. Despite the levelling effect of formulaic style, he talks differently from any other character. Adam Parry rightly drew attention to the dislocations in his speech to Odysseus (IX 308ff.: Parry, 1956), including its strange accumulation of unanswerable questions ('but why should the Argives fight the Trojans . . . ?', 337ff.). Other speeches (such as his speech to Lycaon) show a striking terseness of sentence construction.

Unlike other characters, Achilles is also given to using similes, which in general belong to the expressive repertoire of the narrative, and one of these is particularly noteworthy. The narrator frequently represents the heroes as marauding, inhuman lions, and in his combat with Hector, Achilles sees himself, as opposed to his opponent, in this role. Before they fight, Hector proposes that they agree to one thing: the winner should return the body of the loser to his own people. Achilles refuses: 'Hector, you are mad to talk to me of agreements: there are no oaths of faith between lions and men . . .' (XXII 261–2). For Achilles, as for an omniscient narrator, *he* is the lion and Hector the man. It is significant that when he responds adversely to Priam, in the consciousness of his situation, he springs from the room, again, 'like a lion' (XXIV 572) – which is the last of all the similes in the poem.

Between the killing and mutilation of Hector and the heightened encounter with Priam, Achilles is seen in two different roles. He organises the funeral for Patroclus and he presides at the funeral games. As the cremation ritual is completed, Achilles wails:

As a father wails for his son, when he burns his bones, a son newly married, whose death has brought grief to his unhappy parents, so Achilles wailed for his friend, as he burned his bones, dragging his feet round the pyre, groaning.   (XXIII 222ff.)

Achilles weeps for Patroclus as father for son, as if by some symbolic identification with Priam grieving for Hector, as he will identify with him in XXIV. Then, at the games, Achilles assumes the role of umpire. Quarrels break out among the spectators, and he deals with them: 'No more angry answers or insults, Ajax and Idomeneus: this is not the time or place. You would be furious if anyone else behaved like this . . .' (XXIII 492ff.). Achilles as tactful peacemaker: once again, his response to Priam is anticipated.

In XXII Achilles is a vengeful killer; in XXIV he is a heightened form of humanity, participating in an extraordinary relationship with his enemy, Priam: the instinctive hero of I has been forced into a momentous self-awareness. The characters in the *Iliad* do not, even cannot, show personal development; and yet Achilles' switch from killer to man – *via* his activities in XXIII – looks remarkably like it. Sensitive critics grope for the right answer. Some talk of Achilles' 'maturation', as if it were a process and a natural movement up the pre-ordained ages of man. Macleod speaks of his 'development of character – or better, enlargement of experience and comprehension' – which seems to leave the question in the air, but in any case represents too pious a formula for this particular pilgrim's often unsavoury progress. The truth (we would argue) is that Achilles does, uniquely, 'develop', but that this 'development' is represented not as a process, let alone a natural one, but as a series of responses to experience, most of them excessive. On his first appearance in the *Iliad*, in I before the quarrel, Achilles is courteous and responsible. When Apollo's plague afflicts the Achaeans, it is Achilles who summons an assembly to consider its cause (I 54ff., 84ff.). His hot temper is soon apparent, of course, but so it is in his encounter with Priam. It is as if his 'mature' response to Priam is conceived of as the restoration of a proper emotional balance – almost as in the later Greek theory of humours – without reference to his new consciousness at all. Yet this consciousness is a fact, and a formative one. That Achilles can characterise his present relationship with Priam as 'squatting here at Troy, afflicting you and your children' (XXIV 542) implies a remarkable distance from himself, which the idiomatic and almost dismissively brusque 'squatting' (*hêmai*) seems to enforce. What he undergoes and achieves is unique in the poem and, so far as we know, for some centuries to come.

21 Achilles and heroic ideology

The *Iliad* presents a coherent heroic ideology, which presupposes war. That ideology is celebrated and affirmed by the poem, in that it is what the heroes in general live by, while the poem unquestionably celebrates *them*. At the same time, the supreme hero is Achilles, and it is clear that Achilles is an uncomfortable and even a destructive presence within the heroic world. This paradox has produced much discussion. Where some interpreters (like M. I. Finley) have taken Homer's world to be an unqualified expression of heroic ideology, others (like Redfield) have seen the *Iliad* as a critique of the ideology itself. Let us suggest here that with the glorious, but extreme, hero Achilles at its centre, the poem is so structured as to reveal the negative implications of heroic values *along with* their obvious splendour. The *Iliad* does not read like a studied critique of accepted values – as if Homer was a Brecht, say, a Marxist before his time. The greatest literature, however, as neo-Marxist theorists like Eagleton have pointed out, is wont to subvert the dominant ideological categories that it purports to, and does indeed also, embody: and, thanks to Achilles, the *Iliad* surely does just this.

Achilles' subversive role is nowhere more obvious than when he seems to reject the heroic code in his speech to Odysseus (IX 318ff.). However, the nature of this 'rejection' is strictly qualified. Achilles withdraws from the war in the first place, not out of anti-heroic disaffection with heroic combat itself, but in heroic protest against the dishonour done to him and with a heroic ambition of additional honours at a later date. He originally planned to return in circumstances when the greatest honour (in the shape of gifts) would accrue: he does in fact return in a spirit of revenge, apparently unconcerned with gifts of honour, but determined rather, by this revenge, to win glory, *kléos* (XVIII 121). One aspect of heroic values, therefore, is, to some extent, exchanged for another. And though his 'squatting here at Troy' (XXIV 542) may sound at odds with heroic endeavour as a whole, the consolation of glory, at least, is never rejected. But we must add that by the poem's end this consolation, like so much else, is implicitly qualified. Heroic ideology insists on a special kind of optimism: the quest for glory presupposes a bleak acceptance that this life is all the life we have, but also the hope of a secondary immortality, for the favoured few, through achievement. Yet Achilles, the supreme achiever, sums up his experience of life, not in terms of glory and hope, but through the image of the urns of Zeus. That image promises blessings as well as afflictions, but afflictions predominate and, in particular, nothing is said of any permanent consolation.

We might suppose that, in the context of such a pessimistic summing-up, immortal achievement and the consolation it yields should become yet more precious, but Achilles neither says this nor denies it. A tidy answer misrepresents the poem. Heroic endeavour *and* Achilles' eccentric version of it are both offered as realities. Homer's presentation of war subsumes the heroic attitude, along with others (pp. 61–9). His presentation of Achilles includes both a contribution to heroism and a challenge to it.

22 Conclusions

What makes the *Iliad* a 'landmark of world literature'? Partly the circumstance that it is the first work of Western literature to survive; partly its multifarious influence (pp. 93ff.); but in any case its remarkable inherent qualities.

One of these qualities is balance: a balanced inclusiveness that can make room for opposites, even seemingly incompatible opposites. Again and again our discussion has pointed this way. The poem offers us both a pervasive stylisation and a powerful immediacy, with the two sometimes embodied even in the same elements, such as the generic epithets. It offers us war, but through the similes and Achilles' shield in particular, allows us to glimpse the world of peace which war undermines. Within the orbit of war, we witness its glory *and* its suffering: Hector and his grandeur *and* Andromache and Astyanax and their simplicity. The gods are majestic, but also trivial, even comic: on the one hand, great Zeus holds his gold scales and Hephaestus forges Achilles' magnificent armour; on the other, Zeus is seduced by a crafty Hera and Hephaestus limps across the Olympians' dining-hall. Majestic or trivial, these gods constantly interfere in the heroes' acts of will; and yet they are still acts of will, and human autonomy, though not unaffected, is not obliterated. The *Iliad* impresses us with its heroic ideology: it impresses us too with Achilles' threatened subversion of that ideology. We see life through a heroic perspective: we observe it also through the opposite perspectives of immortal gods and ordinary, anonymous, mortal men.

Perhaps the simplest example of the poem's balance is the parity of status and dignity it establishes between the two sides, Trojans and Achaeans. This is equally apparent whether they engage in external combat, or meet in personal confrontation (above all, in XXIV), or conduct their separate activities. The war *could* have been presented as a matter of Greeks versus foreigners, or even hard Europeans versus degenerate Asiatics, an opposition which was to become a cliché in centuries to come. The Trojans do indeed include a mixture of nationalities (IV 436ff.), and Paris, the author of his people's affliction, has more than a touch of degenerate refinement: he is the sensual protégé of Aphrodite (III 64ff.) who, for all his guilt, treats his situation and the heroic obligations it implies in an almost flippant spirit (VI 339). But Paris' anti-heroics are specifically contrasted with the conduct of Hector (III 30–66, VI 318–68, VI 440–502, 503–25); and Hector is the greatest, therefore the truest, representative of Troy. It is Trojans, not Achaeans, who break 'oaths of faith' (IV 157, VII 351–2), but only in X do we seem to have any generalised moral disparity – feeble Trojans, brave Greeks. It is true that, in the poem as a whole, far more Trojans are killed (about three of them for each Achaean death), and only one of the great deaths is suffered by an Achaean, Patroclus. Against that, the Trojans are accorded all the dignity of the defeated, as any reader of the Andromache scene in VI or the Priam scene in XXIV must agree.

With all its deaths and defeats, the *Iliad* might have been a highly emotive work. The degree of stylisation in the poem, however, tends to keep the reader at a distance where feelings of emotional involvement are less aroused than the nature of the material would lead one to expect, especially in the narrative. By comparison with many writers (Virgil, for one) Homer strikes us as impersonal and 'objective' (Brooks Otis). Yet it is not that emotion is ever absent from the poem. It is rather that the author does not allow emotion to be determinative: he is like his gods, who pity Sarpedon or Hector, but resist the temptation to interfere. Explicit comments in the narrative that abandon the narrator's impersonal stance are few and modest: Patroclus pressed on after the Trojans blindly, 'in his innocence': he should have done what Achilles told him (XVI 684ff.). Normally it is only Homer's characters who express feelings, as they do with great freedom in their speeches, whereas the author allows our feelings to form themselves in response to the specifics of the situation. He does not press on us his admiration of Helen's beauty: he conveys it through the grudging compliments from the old men of Troy (III 156ff.). He does not tell us how absorbing the fighting is: he shows us the gods watching, as we watch. He does not inject emotion into Hector's farewell to Andromache or his flight from Achilles: he embodies it in a helmet and a line of washing-tanks (pp. 57–61, 66).

Distance, however, is not preserved uniformly. In exceptional cases it is shortened, as it is with Hector's flight from Achilles (pp. 57f.), or, more commonly, it is reduced just enough to permit a refined pathos. A representative example is the death of Lycaon at the hands of Achilles (XXI 34–135). Here the emotion is brought into play by a contrast between the narrator's perspective, Lycaon's supplication ('pity me . . .', 74ff.), and Achilles' cold gloating ('lie there among the fish . . .', 122ff.). The narrator's 'necrology' is in itself matter-of-fact: 'he lay stretched out, front down, and his dark blood poured out and wet the ground' (118–19) The narrator, however, has already explained Lycaon's peculiar circumstances. He had been captured once before by a more merciful Achilles and sent to Lemnos for a ransom; then 'he had eleven days' joy of his friends after he arrived back from Lemnos, but on the twelfth a god put him back into the hands of Achilles, who was to send him to the house of Hades, unwilling though he was to go' (45ff.). Similar effects are associated with some of the contrastive similes (pp. 66f.).

Of all the oppositions just mentioned, the one between stylisation and immediacy is the most far-reaching. 'Immediacy' evokes naked, protean experience; 'stylisation' suggests experience mediated by patterning, convention, fixed form. Immediacy permits change; stylisation militates against it. Stylisation, therefore, is static, immediacy dynamic, and the co-presence of static and dynamic elements in the poem is evident on all levels, from the stylistic upwards. We see it on the level of structure, where there is a progressive plot, developing the logic of events (that is, the consequences of Achilles' behaviour), yet also a rich texture of prolonged moments – similes, speeches, situations (pp. 34f., 50–3). On most levels the static predominates, as it does in the presentation of character. With the exception of Achilles, the characters are solid, stable figures, incapable of change, except such change as is associated with physical maturing and physical ageing (pp. 75f.). It is no coincidence that the same is true of the *Iliad's* sense of history. There is no perception of historical development as such, but of a cyclical rise and fall: communities come and go (e.g. II 116ff.), as do the individuals who belong to them, like leaves in season (VI 146ff.).

In themselves, the static qualities of Homer's poetry seem alien to us. The harmonious, repetitious regularity of it all is more akin to ritual than we expect of literature. Yet as we read, the ritualism seems appropriate and right. Why should this be so? Above all, because of the coherence of this poetic system with the content of the poem. For it is not only the presentation that has a predominantly ritualistic character: it is also the life presented in the poem, the human experience it deals in. Here too, we modern readers are in alien country. We are of course used to the ritualisation of certain aspects of life. We accept the idea that games should have fixed rules, that public meetings should be conducted in a formal way, that prayers should have conventional forms. But our world has no equivalent to the stereotyped supplications and lamentations in the *Iliad*, or its elaborate code of hospitality and gift-giving (on which, for instance, the Glaucus–Diomedes scene depends, p. 25) or, again, its ritualised fighting. The heroes kill, but their killings are regulated by ceremony. One aims a spear; the other waits his turn. Menelaus declares his intention to attack, Euphorbus his intention to defend (XVII 9–32).

The combat of Paris and Menelaus in III involves umpires (314ff.), oaths and sacrifices (245ff.). The duel of Hector and Ajax in VII is called off for bad light by heralds from the two sides (273ff.), upon which the combatants exchange gifts (299ff.). Achilles' mutilation of Hector is exceptional: for all the wild, predatory motions in the similes, there is very little raw savagery in the *Iliad*.

Homer's ritualistic gift-givings, lamentations, supplications, prayers, public meetings, games and fighting conducted like games, are all communal events. They are not, primarily, personal experiences through which an individual explores his identity. They are more like social occasions – even the fighting and killing – through which the whole community translates its sense of the stabilities of life into a celebration.

The *Iliad* is primarily celebratory, not exploratory. It presents the unchanging surface of experience, rather than the depths where nothing is constant. Every ritual act, every repeated generic epithet, every stylised gesture or conventional form of words celebrates the regularity and harmony of experience. Our modern Western world is predominantly exploratory; therefore it is suspicious of rituals, eager to get behind conventions, prone to misunderstand the logic of celebration. We value plain utility or else personal integrity, which depends on a person's individual choices and those particular interactions with others which we call 'relationships'; we query the value of kinship or patriotism, where no personal choice is involved; we may interpret crimes according to the nature of the crime committed, but we then re-interpret them according to the intentions of the criminal; we often value achievement more by the scale of the effort than by the qualities of the thing achieved. We feel impelled to go below the surface. With our vast knowledge of different cultures, we compare ours with others and ask, 'could it be better?'; with our consciousness of ourselves, we look at life and ask, 'what for?' We want 'not a having and a resting, but a growing and a becoming', in Matthew Arnold's words.

The celebratory basis of the *Iliad* is shown up negatively in its lack of interest in deep causality, fate, ultimate 'explanations'. It is epitomised as positively as one could wish in the Hector–Andromache scene, the 'lovers' farewell', where the 'love' is a matter of a husband's and a wife's *belonging*. It is no accident that the simple and very common Homeric word for 'beloved', *phílos*, is also the word for 'one's own': 'relationship' here is static.

Nevertheless, the *Iliad* still has a prominent exploratory aspect: the disturbing logic of its events and what that logic means for Achilles. *His* reactions certainly involve a 'becoming', even if we hesitate quite to speak of development. His reconciliation with Priam, above all, is exploratory. Priam has defied convention by coming to him (XXIV 505–6); and as a host, Achilles must invent special procedures to deal with him (582ff., 650ff.). His articulation of the laws of existence in the image of the urns of Zeus (525ff.) is as close as the *Iliad* ever comes to openly exploring the meaning of life. And yet even here 'the having and the resting' are still strongly in evidence. When Priam and Achilles weep, they weep as sufferers stripped to their inner core which they now bare to each other. But they weep not for each other, despite their new kinship in suffering: Priam weeps for his own son, Achilles for his own father 'and now again for Patroclus' (509ff.). And when all is said and done, the whole episode retains a ceremonial basis: the formal exchange of a body for a ransom.

Modern interpreters of the *Iliad* like to relate it to tragedy. The poem was indeed destined to be a formative influence on Greek tragedy (p. 94), but in itself the comparison is misplaced. The reader of the *Iliad* is like a spectator, but hardly a spectator of a tragic drama: reading (or, presumably, hearing) the *Iliad* is like watching sport. In many ways, Homer's characters are more like players on the field than players on a stage. We learn to know these great performers, but (except for Achilles) not as explored individuals. In their interactions and inter-relations, they are all quite different players, but (except for Achilles) they follow rules, and we know them only on these terms. Their great configurations are like great sporting contests. The gods watch them in just such a spirit, and so do we. The gods in fact help us to determine our response, and the author gives us specific encouragement to respond in this way:

> past the washing-tanks they ran, one in flight, one in pursuit behind. It was a fine man in flight in front, but a far better man in pursuit behind: swift pursuit, for it was not a beast of sacrifice or a bull's hide that they

were striving for, such as men have for prizes in the footrace, but it was for the life of horse-taming Hector that they ran. Just as prize-winning hooved horses canter round the turn for a great prize, a cauldron or a woman, <in the games held> for a dead man, so these two circled three times round Priam's city with swift feet, and all the gods were watching.

(XXII 157–66)

The simile prefigures the funeral games of XXIII, and those games surely constitute one of the representative moments of the *Iliad*. The games tend to be vaguely ignored by modern critics as a distraction from the poem's 'real' issues. On the contrary, they represent a situation in which the heroes appear as their 'real' selves.

If the *Iliad* impresses us with its balanced inclusiveness, this is not to say that nothing is excluded from it. In fact the contents and elements of the poem are determined according to a precise sense of relevance. For the sake of coherence, both poetic and ideological, some of these elements (like the pared-down settings) are strictly controlled, while certain areas of experience are excluded altogether, such as the dark religion of the Dionysiac and chthonic cults or, again, romantic love. The poem concentrates on its own coherent action and the general, or universal, experiences that it stylises and recreates. We and the gods watch a particular series of happenings in one place and time: 'other parts of the world hardly play a role, other experiences of other times are almost ignored' (Vivante). Related material, if brought in at all, is brought in, without relaxing the concentration, as subordinate to the action. The material evoking the start and scale of the Trojan war (especially in II-III) is incorporated in this way. There is no sense of digression. But in accordance with the principle of relevance, the background of the Trojan cycle is suppressed, even the momentous and colourful judgement of Paris (mentioned only at XXIV 25–30). Fully independent mythology is generally admitted only for analogies offered by the characters themselves, who occasionally appeal to earlier sagas or generations of heroes as a standard for action. So it is with Nestor's stories of his own youth (like XI 670ff.) and Phoenix's cautionary tale of Meleager (IX 524ff.). Yet even here it has been argued (by Willcock, 1964) that such paradigms may actually involve *ad hoc* invention for the sake of the parallel: the apparently 'independent' material may be nothing of the kind.

In the *Iliad* everything belongs: the poem is an organic whole in senses undreamed of by Aristotle. Mythic idiom belongs with religious ideology, stylised idiom with ritualised behaviour, values with physical facts. Above all, neither the author nor his characters, even Achilles, evoke any appreciable sense of alienation between themselves and their world, any serious wish, such as is already visible in some early Greek poetry, that perhaps the world might be other than it is; and the homogeneity of the poem is perfectly attuned to this outlook.

Chapter 3

The *Iliad* and world literature

23 The after-life of the *Iliad*

It would be a formidable task to attempt a full account of the 'after-life' of the work that inaugurates Western literature. That would involve relating the poem to its many changing interpretations, assessing its use to the Western literary tradition over three millennia, and placing it against all the poetry and prose in many languages that descends from it indirectly. Nor could such an account be a coherent one. For example, part of the use that the *Iliad* was put to in classical Greece — represented, for instance, by its influence on Greek religion (p. 26) – belongs to the history of ancient culture or ideology rather than to literary history in the modern sense. Then again, much notable interpretation of the poem has focused not on its literary significance, but on its technical features or its hypothetical genesis. This is particularly true of ancient Alexandrian scholarship and of the work of the last two centuries in the wake of Wolf, then of Milman Parry (pp. 8, 14ff.). By contrast, the readings characteristic of the Renaissance and the Enlightenment, from the sixteenth century to the eighteenth, present the *Iliad* specifically as literature, but literature in the perspective of Rome: they usually take the form of theories of epic which acclaim Virgil's *Aeneid* and critiques of 'Homer' (meaning *Odyssey* as well as *Iliad*) which bemoan Homer's failure to anticipate Virgilian norms. Even a short list of interpretative insights – from Aristotle to Matthew Arnold, from Longinus to Simone Weil, from Pope to Parry – would be too long and too diverse to discuss briefly. All that can be attempted here is a sketch of the poem's influence within the particular literary tradition that it helped to shape.

In the first place, Homer – the undifferentiated author of the *Iliad* and the *Odyssey* – laid down the fundamental, pan-Hellenic norms of serious Greek poetry, whether epic, dramatic, or lyric (*cf.* p. 3): an idiom elevated above the colloquial, a hero elevated above the common man, the extreme situation as the hero's natural arena, and a large-scale, metrically consistent, unified structure as the suitable medium for any ambitious literary work. And thanks to Latin imitations, such remained the premises of Western poetry until the iconoclasm of the Romantics and the evolution of new modes of literature associated with the rise of the nineteenth-century realist novel. The most immediate legatee of these tendencies, however, was Greek tragedy, which also learned from the Homeric technique of direct speech and – this time, with a particular indebtedness to the *Iliad* – from the epic presentation of destructive conflict. Certainly for many critics – from Plato (who saw Homer as the 'pathfinder' of tragedy, *Republic* 598d) to George Steiner (in whose *Death of Tragedy* the *Iliad* becomes 'the primer of tragic art') – this connection has seemed a special one.

There are also works that look back more self-consciously to the *Iliad*, works as different as *Rhesus* and *Tom Jones*: a tragedy ascribed to Euripides, but probably belonging to the fourth century B.C., which dramatises part of the 'Doloneia' (X) and is the only extant tragedy to re-use material from the *Iliad* (here at least Homer's heirs used their legacy sparingly); and Fielding's mock-epic novel, published in 1749, which uses Homeric heroics as foil for the comic diversities of the contemporary world and for which the poet of the *Iliad* (and others) are 'so many wealthy squires, from whom we, the poor of Parnassus, claim an immemorial custom of taking whatever we can come at' (*Tom Jones* XII, 1). A different category consists of classic translations and new literature stimulated by their appearance. There is, for instance, the famous German version by Johann Heinrich Voss (1793) which – in conjunction with Wolf's momentous *Introduction to Homer*, two years later (p. 8) – stimulated the production of Goethe's unfinished *Achilleis* (begun in 1799); and (a century before Pope's great English translation) the bold version by Shakespeare's contemporary, Chapman, the first parts of which (I–II, VII–XI) came out in

1598 and prompted the duel of Hector and Ajax and the character
of Thersites in Shakespeare's *Troilus and Cressida* (? 1602).

24 The *Iliad*, the *Odyssey*, the *Aeneid* and *Paradise Lost*

But the specific influence of the *Iliad* is found at its most significant
within the genre of epic poetry itself. Apart from the various national traditions of heroic poetry, such as gave rise to the Old English
Beowulf and the medieval romances, the long sequence of European
narrative poems from early Greece to the modern period represents a
coherent series whose norms are those the *Iliad* established. Within
this series, the *Iliad's* mechanisms and technical features – generic
epithets and invocations to the Muse, 'extended' similes and divine
apparatus – all become predictable conventions. Other, larger, features of the poem likewise acquire a definitive status: conflict between two parties, double perspective of narrative and direct speech
and, above all, scale. And scale – meaning both the great length
of the composition and the grandeur of the events depicted in it –
remains the one characteristic of the traditional genre still assumed
in the modern sense of 'epic' as promoted by Hollywood.

Above all, the series of epic poems includes three other 'landmarks of world literature' which in their different ways look back to
the *Iliad*, taking it as their point of departure for new developments
which would have been inconceivable without the *Iliad* behind
them. These are: the *Odyssey* (*c.* 700), perhaps and perhaps not the
work of the 'Homer' to whom we ascribe the *Iliad*; Virgil's *Aeneid*,
begun in 30–29 B.C. and not quite finished when its author died
eleven years later; and Milton's *Paradise Lost*, published in 1667.

The *Odyssey*, we assume (pp. 3ff.), was conceived as a monumental epic on the model of the *Iliad*; and deriving from the same oral
context, as it doubtless does, it in any case shares many of the *Iliad's*
characteristics, large and small. At the same time, if offers, in effect,
an alternative model of what world literature might be. The *Odyssey*
is about one hero, or rather, one very human *man*, as its first word,
ándra, makes clear: *ándra moi énnepe, Moûsa, polútropon . . .*: 'the

man of many wiles – Muse, tell me of him . . .'. And with this single 'wily' hero, whose quest we follow through a variety of times and places; with its excursions into the realms of romance – a giant, a witch, a princess waiting for her prince – but also its portrayal of the hard reality of mundane Ithaca; with a new world of character study and domestic relationships; with a new range of emotions and values, from the guile of Odysseus himself to the delicate irony with which the princess Nausicaa's unspoken hopes of a husband are presented: with all of this the *Odyssey* lays down the groundwork for the novel, as surely as the *Iliad* does for tragedy. The distance of the *Odyssey* from the *Iliad* (and from tragedy) is summed up by its substitution of a conflict between good Odysseus and evil suitors for the older poem's moral balance of Trojans and Achaeans – and equally by its related conversion of the *Iliad*'s divine spectators into superior moral forces which ensure that the good Odysseus wins in the end.

Yet the *Odyssey* continues to point to the *Iliad*, and not merely to their common inheritance, by a series of evocations of the Iliadic war and its Iliadic heroes. In the underworld, Odysseus meets, among others, Agamemnon, Achilles and Ajax (*Odyssey* XI); elsewhere we hear reminiscences from the living, Nestor, Menelaus and Helen (*Odyssey* III–IV). Actual duplication of material is meticulously avoided, but the result of the evocations is that (in the words of one ancient critic): 'the *Odyssey* is virtually an epilogue to the *Iliad*: "There lies warlike Ajax, there Achilles, there Patroclus . . ."' (*Odyssey* III 109f.: 'Longinus', *On the Sublime* ix 12).

If the *Iliad* and *Odyssey* belong together – as likes and unlikes, complements and opposites – so in another way do the *Iliad*, the *Aeneid* and *Paradise Lost*. Where the *Iliad* is predominantly celebratory, the great epics of Virgil and Milton have overt ambitions to explore. The *Aeneid* is concerned not to present life, but to give meaning to it. The poem sets out to articulate the destiny of the Roman nation, by relating the contemporary world of civil war and empire to the past, both historical and literary; and these two pasts become one in the person of Aeneas, refugee from Homer's Troy and (by divine commandment) 'pious' founder of a new Troy, to be called Rome. Aeneas is the suffering creator of Rome, and the great moral issue explored by the *Aeneid* is the value of such suffering.

Just as the *Aeneid* connects Rome and Homer, so *Paradise Lost* brings together Christianity and the whole literary tradition epitomised by the *Aeneid* and the *Iliad*. Milton's celebrated aim is to 'justify the ways of God to men' (*Paradise Lost* I 26). The implications of this exploratory project make it plain how his epic presupposes *Aeneid* and *Iliad* together. The 'ways of God', like the ways of Virgil's cosmos, are to be justified by an articulation of destiny, but now the destiny belongs not to a nation, but to mankind as a whole; and the new empire to which suffering leads is the spiritual empire of Christ. That empire lies in the future as a hope. In the past are the events which make that hope necessary and derive their deepest meaning from it: the fall of man and its cause in the rebellion against God by Satan and his league of discontented angels. The spring and the central figure of Milton's epic is not God, nor indeed Adam and Eve, the humans who fall, but Satan, whose status is between the two. He is himself a kind of divinity, yet he is also, like man, a victim of the divine, and as such a suitable 'hero', albeit not in the moral sense. But where Milton's God is naturally a Christian god, his Arch-fiend Satan, as a rebel against the Christian god, can only be a pagan. He is a pagan god and (as central figure) a pagan hero – like the gods of the *Iliad* and like the Achaean and Trojan heroes they resemble. No more powerful presentation of pagan gods and pagan heroes was available to Milton than the presentation in the *Iliad*. Accordingly, he looks back to the *Iliad* for his inspiration, and invests his Satan with the proud magnificence of Homer's combative deities and equally with the lineaments of his heroes and *their* magnificent pride: 'All is not lost – the unconquerable will' (*Paradise Lost* I 106). Satan is to God rather as Homer's Achilles might be to Virgil's 'pious' Aeneas.

The particular 'imitations' of the *Iliad* in the two later epics are many, and include set pieces like the funeral games in *Aeneid* V and the battle of the gods (angels *versus* rebel angels) in *Paradise Lost* VI. More revealing for the relationships as just outlined are the programmatic allusions to the *Iliad* in their opening lines. The *Iliad* begins with its reference to Achilles' feud with Agamemnon – *mênin áeide theá* ('wrath sing, goddess'). The narrator then poses and answers a question that gets the action of the poem under way: 'which of the gods brought them into conflict? Apollo, son of Leto and Zeus, in anger with the king...' (I 8–9). In its famous first words, *arma virumque cano* ('arms and the man I sing'), the *Aeneid* evokes the sense of Homer's *mēnin* (and, in the next breath, the *Odyssey*'s first word, *ándra*). A few verses later, Virgil duly evokes Homer's factual question and answer, but in his new spirit. Aeneas, the 'man' of the opening phrase, was cast out of Troy and suffered *Iunonis ob iram*, 'thanks to the anger of the goddess Juno' (the Roman Hera): *tantaene animis caelestibus irae*, 'are gods in heaven capable of such rancour?' (*Aeneid* I 1–4, 11). The reformulated question and answer points to the agonising moral question the *Aeneid* is to explore in the very act of evoking the epic to which such agonies and such explorations are so alien.

Milton's opening phrases succeed in bringing *Iliad* and *Aeneid* into a simultaneous presence: 'Of man's first disobedience... Sing, heavenly Muse...' (*Paradise Lost* I 1, 6). 'Man' offers the sense of Virgil's *virum*, but the sound of Homer's *mēnin*: the sense of *mēnin* is implicit rather in the 'disobedience'. And the double presence is maintained when Milton comes to the question – 'Who first seduced them [our grand parents] to that foul revolt?' – and the answer: 'The infernal serpent: he it was whose guile, / Stirred up with envy and revenge, deceived / The mother of mankind, what time his pride / Had cast him out from heaven...' (*Paradise Lost* I 33ff.). Satan's 'revenge' and 'pride' recall Homer's Apollo and also his Achilles; he is 'cast out from heaven' as Virgil's Aeneas was from Troy; and his revenge on 'the mother of mankind' duly leads to the second 'casting-out', the expulsion of Adam and Eve from Paradise. Milton's justification of 'the ways of God' begins.

Such pointed allusions are themselves symptomatic of exploratory literature. They invite the reader to make comparisons and think of alternatives, to look at a new conception of life and to place it by relating it to earlier conceptions. The conception of life offered by the *Iliad* seems, by comparison, self-sufficient.

Guide to further reading

Items marked with an asterisk (*) require no knowledge of Greek or else not enough to put off a determined, but Greekless, reader.

(a) Bibliography

The number of publications relevant to Homer in general, and the *Iliad* in particular, is huge. What follows is a short-list of works of particular importance or representative interest. For further bibliography, with critical discussion, see *R. B. Rutherford, *Homer* (Oxford 1996) (*Greece and Rome* New Surveys in the Classics, 26), pp. 105–7, and *D. L. Cairns (ed.), *Oxford Readings in Homer's Iliad* (Oxford 2001), pp. 1–56.

(b) Editions, commentaries, translations

The standard Greek edition without commentary is *Homeri Ilias*, ed. T. W. Allen, 3 vols. (London 1931).

English commentaries on the Greek: *The Iliad: A Commentary*, ed. G. S. Kirk, J. B. Hainsworth, R. Janko, M. W. Edwards and N. J. Richardson (6 vols., Cambridge 1985–93) (a major work of scholarship; the later volumes are especially rewarding); *The Iliad of Homer*, ed. M. M. Willcock (2 vols., London 1978–84) (concise and reliable); *Homer, Iliad, Books VIII and IX*, ed. C. H. Wilson (Warminster 1996) (with facing translation); *Homer, Iliad IX*, ed. J. Griffin (Cambridge 1995); *Homer, Iliad, Book XXIV*, ed. C. W. Macleod (Cambridge 1982). Note also * J. C. Hogan, *A Guide to the Iliad* (New York 1979), and *M. M. Willcock, *A Companion to the Iliad* (Chicago and London 1976), which provide notes on Fitzgerald's and Lattimore's translations (see below) respectively.

Of the translations discussed in the text (section 14), the one most likely to be read today as a translation of Homer is *The Iliad*, tr. Robert Fitzgerald (New York 1974) (less successful, in the present writer's judgement, than Fitzgerald's version of the *Odyssey*, 1961). *The Iliad*, tr. A. Lang, W. Leaf and E. Myers (rev. edn, London 1914), is not widely available, unlike *The Iliad of Homer*, tr. Alexander Pope (1715–20), often reprinted, and most comprehensively edited in The Twickenham Edition of Pope's Complete Poems, vols. VII–VIII, ed. M. Mack (London and New Haven 1967). For better or worse, many readers will want a 'close' version, more concerned with denotative specifics than with the effect of Homer's Greek. The best-known verse translation of this kind is *The Iliad of Homer*, tr. Richmond Lattimore (Chicago 1951) (on which see Mason, below); the best-known prose equivalent is *Homer, The Iliad*, tr. M. Hammond (Harmondsworth 1987) (on which see my review in *Journal of Hellenic Studies* 110 (1990), 204–5). *Homer, Iliad*, tr. S. Lombardo (Indianapolis 1997), is roughly in the Fitzgerald tradition, with (even) less stylised English (cf. my review in the *Times Literary Supplement* 4942 (19 December 1997), 3–4).

*Matthew Arnold's long essay, *On Translating Homer* (1861), like Pope's translation, which (among others) it discusses, is available in various editions. Anyone seriously interested in the question of translation should read *H. A. Mason, *To Homer through Pope* (London 1972), the anthology *Homer in English*, ed. George Steiner (Harmondsworth 1996), and *John Dryden's version of 'The First Book of Homer's *Iliad*' (1700), a precursor in some ways of Pope's translation, which is intermittently brilliant. Poetic translation shades off into creative imitation. The most powerful of recent responses of this kind to the *Iliad* is Christopher Logue's series of versions of sections of the poem, from *Patrocleia* (1962) to *The Husbands* (1994). In this connection see *S. Underwood, *English Translators of Homer: From George Chapman to Christopher Logue* (Plymouth 1998).

(c) Background

The items listed under this heading are especially relevant to the topics discussed in Chapter 1 (and will often be found to take different positions, or pursue different approaches, from mine). General: Rutherford, *Homer* (under (a) above); *R. L. Fowler (ed.), *The Cambridge Companion to Homer* (Cambridge 2004); I. Morris and B. Powell (eds.), *A New Companion to Homer* (Leyden 1997); G. S. Kirk, *The Songs of Homer* (Cambridge 1962). Historical/sociological context: *M. I. Finley, *The World of Odysseus* (2nd edn, Harmondsworth 1979); *Oswyn Murray, *Early Greece* (London 1980). On Parry, formulae and related issues: Norman Austin, *Archery at the Dark of the Moon* (Berkeley 1975), pp. 11–80; G. S. Kirk (ed.), *Language and Background of Homer* (Cambridge 1964); Adam Parry (ed.), *The Making of Homeric Verse: The Collected Papers of Milman Parry* (Oxford 1971); Adam Parry, *The Language of Achilles and Other Papers*, ed. H. Lloyd-Jones

(Oxford 1989); Hainsworth in vol. 3 of Kirk (etc.), *The Iliad: A Commentary* (see (b) above), pp. 1–31. Differing approaches to the status/'development', therefore also dating, of the Homeric poems: G. Nagy, *Poetry as Performance: Homer and Beyond* (Cambridge 1996); *B. Graziosi, *Inventing Homer: The Early Reception of Epic* (Cambridge 2002); R. Janko, *Homer, Hesiod and the Hymns* (Cambridge 1982). A representative statement of fundamentalist oralism: *J. M. Foley, *Homer's Traditional Art* (University Park, Pa 1999). Important correctives to any such fundamentalism: *Ruth Finnegan, *Oral Poetry* (Cambridge 1977); *Rosalind Thomas, *Literacy and Orality in Ancient Greece* (Cambridge 1992). Homer and early art: K. F. Johansen, *The Iliad in Early Greek Art* (Copenhagen 1967); *A. Snodgrass, *Homer and the Artists: Text and Picture in Early Greek Art* (Cambridge 1998).

(d) Literary interpretation

First, three brief, brilliant, contrasting characterisations: *Erich Auerbach, 'Odysseus' Scar', ch. 1 of *Mimesis*, tr. W. Trask (Princeton 1953), repr. in e.g. *Homer*, ed. G. Steiner and R. Fagles (Englewood Cliffs, NJ 1962), on Homeric realism; *Simone Weil, 'L'Iliade, ou le poème de la force' (1940), in *La source grecque* (Paris 1952), tr. as *The Iliad or the Poem of Force* by Mary McCarthy (New York 1945) and as 'The *Iliad*, Poem of Might' by E. C. Geissbuhler in S. Weil, *Intimations of Christianity among the Ancient Greeks* (London 1957), a wonderful, if perilously Christian, reading of the poem's destructive conflicts; a necessary corrective to Weil, the opening paragraphs of *Friedrich Nietzsche, 'Homer's Contest' (1872) (tr. e.g. *W. Kaufmann, *The Portable Nietzsche* (rev. edn, New York 1968), pp. 32–5), on the rationale of those conflicts, along with Nietzsche's classic representation of Homer as an 'Apolline' artist in sections 1–6 of *The Birth of Tragedy* (also 1872, various translations available).

Illuminating modern criticism from various standpoints: I. J. F. De Jong, *Narrators and Focalizers: The Presentation of the Story of the Iliad* (Amsterdam 1987); *A. Ford, *Homer: The Poetry of the Past* (Ithaca, NY 1992); *J. Griffin, *Homer on Life and Death* (Oxford 1980); M. Lynn-George, *Epos: Word, Narrative and the Iliad* (London 1988); C. Moulton, *Similes in the Homeric Poems* (Göttingen 1977); *M. Mueller, *The Iliad* (London 1984); Brooks Otis, *Virgil: A Study in Civilized Poetry* (Oxford 1963), pp. 41–96 (contrasts 'objective' Homer with 'subjective' Virgil); Adam Parry, 'The Language of Achilles', *Transactions and Proceedings of the American Philological Association* 87 (1956), 1–7 (repr. in Kirk, *Language and Background*, and Adam Parry, *The Language of Achilles and Other Papers*, both in (c) above); *P. Pucci, *The Song of the Sirens: Essays on Homer* (Lanham, Md 1998); *L. Slatkin, *The Power of*

Thetis: Allusion and Interpretation in the Iliad (Berkeley 1991); O. Taplin, 'The Shield of Achilles within the *Iliad'*, *Greece and Rome* 27 (1980), 1–21 (repr. in Cairns, *Oxford Readings*, in (a) above); *O. Taplin, *Homeric Soundings: The Shaping of the Iliad* (Oxford 1992); *P. Vivante, *The Homeric Imagination: A Study of Homer's Poetic Perception of Reality* (Bloomington 1970); M. M. Willcock, 'Mythological Paradeigma in the *Iliad'*, *Classical Quarterly* 14 (1964), 141–54 (repr. in Cairns, *Oxford Readings*, under (a) above). Other worthwhile essays in Cairns, *Oxford Readings* (under (a) above); Fowler, *Cambridge Companion* (under (c) above); *J. Wright (ed.), *Essays on the Iliad* (Bloomington 1978). Two important studies in German: Karl Reinhardt, *Die Ilias und ihr Dichter*, ed. U. Hölscher (Göttingen 1961); Wolfgang Schadewaldt, *Von Homers Welt und Werk* (4th edn, Stuttgart 1965). Diverse thoughts on the poem's ideological presuppositions or constructions: H. Fränkel, *Early Greek Poetry and Philosophy* (Oxford 1975); R. P. Martin, *The Language of Heroes: Speech and Performance in the Iliad* (Princeton 1989); G. Nagy, *The Best of the Achaeans: Concepts of the Hero in Archaic Greek Poetry* (Baltimore 1979); *J. M. Redfield, *Nature and Culture in the Iliad* (2nd edn, Chicago 1994); J. Haubold, *Homer's People: Epic Poetry and Social Formation* (Cambridge 2000), and *D. Lateiner, *Sardonic Smile: Nonverbal Behavior in Homeric Epic* (Ann Arbor 1998), are both more illuminating on the *Odyssey*, but relevant to Homer as a whole.

(e) After-life

General: *H. Clarke, *Homer's Readers* (East Brunswick, NJ 1981); *R. Lamberton and J. Keaney (eds.), *Homer's Ancient Readers* (Princeton 1992); *K. C. King, *Achilles: Paradigms of the War Hero from Homer to the Middle Ages* (Berkeley 1987); *J. L. Myres, *Homer and His Critics* (ed. D. Gray, London 1958). On Homer and later literary epic: *D. Quint, *Epic and Empire: Politics and Generic Form from Virgil to Milton* (Princeton 1993) (ostensibly on post-Homeric epic, in fact illuminates the whole 'epic' tradition from Homer to Eisenstein); *C. S. Lewis, *A Preface to Paradise Lost* (Oxford 1942) (memorable, if sometimes naive, placing of the 'primary epic' of Homer against the 'secondary epic' of Virgil and Milton); *K. W. Gransden, *Virgil's Iliad* (Cambridge 1984); *C. Martindale, *John Milton and the Transformation of Ancient Epic* (London 1986). Relevant discussion also in Mueller (under (d) above) and (given that translation is a form of reception) likewise in Arnold, Mason, Steiner and Underwood (under (c) above); further essays also in Fowler, *Cambridge Companion* (under (c) above), including one by the present author, *'The *Odyssey* and Its Explorations', pursuing the contrastive relationship of *Iliad* and *Odyssey*, with which compare *R. B. Rutherford, 'From the *Iliad* to the *Odyssey'*, in Cairns, *Oxford Readings* (under (a) above).

The important, but often elusive relation between Homer, esp. the *Iliad*, and Greek tragedy awaits adequate treatment. Some pointers and scattered observations in: P. E. Easterling, 'The Tragic Homer', *Bulletin of the Institute of Classical Studies* 31 (1984), 1–8; *S. Goldhill, *Reading Greek Tragedy* (Cambridge 1986), pp. 138–67; *J. Herington, *Poetry into Drama: Early Tragedy and the Greek Poetic Tradition* (Berkeley 1985); R. Garner, *From Homer to Tragedy: The Art of Allusion in Greek Poetry* (London 1990); *P. W. Rose, *Sons of the Gods, Children of Earth: Ideology and Literary Form in Ancient Greece* (Ithaca, NY 1992); *R. Seaford, *Reciprocity and Ritual: Homer and Tragedy in the Developing City-State* (Oxford 1994). Reception of Homer in Western (post-antique) visual art is likewise short of adequate discussion; *M. R. Scherer, *The Legends of Troy in Art and Literature* (Yale 1964), is a start.